THE
DESIGNER'S COOKBOOK

12
COLORS
12
MENUS

PRESTEL

MUNICH · LONDON · NEW YORK

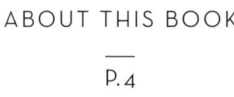

FOREWORD

Too often we sleep walk through our lives.

We exist, but somehow fail to be active participants in our daily routine. Take the last meal you ate. Why did you compose it in the way that you did? Chances are it was arbitrary: choosing a sandwich from the display in a café or opening the refrigerator and finishing last night's leftovers. Some days, eating becomes routine, almost monotonous.

The American writer Paul Auster knows a thing or two about vividly challenging the mundane. In his novels, characters are often obsessive, unorthodox and either ensnared by or frighteningly free of everyday routines. Take Maria Turner from the novel *Leviathan*, who was inspired by the French conceptual artist Sophie Calle. In the novel, Maria's work is all about experimenting with consciously created constraints as a way to enrich her daily life: she spends days under the spell of a single letter of the alphabet; she photographs hotel rooms before they are cleaned to try to understand the life of the departed guest; and she eats meals of only one color each day of the week. It was this last constraint that inspired this book: what would a cookbook for Maria's monochrome diet days look like? And what would it feel like to cook and eat meals of just one color?

In this book, the menus insist that you create meals in only one color, be that white or violet or red or dark green. These are recipes that do not allow for the arbitrary and they demand meticulous attention to detail. Cooking in this way establishes firm limits and insists on a reliance on structure, but when you try it you may find that working within constraints can widen your horizons and bring the mundane vividly to life. And I think that's why Maria Turner would like this book: it sets strict boundaries, but in the end results in greater creativity in the everyday.

TRISH LORENZ

ABOUT THIS BOOK

Food prepared in one single color? How does that taste? Well, after two years of cooking monochromatic menus, we can definitely say: it doesn't just look remarkable, it tastes remarkable, too!

Oh, and another thing: one-color cooking is not just a unique experience, it is an invitation to experiment with unknown flavors and ingredients. What's more, it is a challenge for our taste buds and will shake up our usual methods of preparing food – methods we have practiced and honed over the years. Now is the time to sample alternative ingredients, try new ways of creating familiar recipes and try new ways of presenting traditional meals.

In the Red Menu, for example, what do you think could be substituted for green basil in a red tomato soup? Or, in the Green Menu, what ingredient could turn a brownie into a green brownie? The results are surprising twists on trusted recipes, which, at the same time, create an unspoiled visual highlight.

How would you imagine black food to taste? Do colors automatically determine flavors? Believe it or not, a great tasting menu is possible in any color, whether hearty or light, sweet or savory. We decided that the only way to truly embrace this idea would be to create a series of four-course menus, each menu including three beverages.

So, how did we come up with the recipes? All ingredients are meant to be fresh and regional in order to guarantee flavor, ripeness, and availability. First, we decided to have one menu for each month of the year and then we assigned a color to each month: vigorous colors in summer; faded, "non-colors" in winter; softer hues in spring; and richer tones in fall.

Next, we made a list of all possible ingredients and their corresponding colors. We determined the main courses first, and then chose complimentary appetizers, side dishes, desserts and drinks. Sometimes we based the recipes on familiar meals we loved and adjusted them according to color. But we also experimented and improvised with brand new dishes. We tried many different versions until we were happy with the taste and the color presentation.

The menus proved to be a great deal of work, so we always cooked as a team. Sometimes we were eight cooks, sometimes only three. Each menu was prepared in a day, in an eleven square meter kitchen. We relied on our improvised photo studio to photograph all of the raw ingredients and then the finished dishes.

But no matter how much we describe the recipes, you won't be able to fully appreciate these meals until you try them for yourself. So, go ahead and get inspired – bon appétit!

COMMENTS ON THE RECIPES AND PREPARATION

We prepared the menus in a very small kitchen with simple equipment. Some utensils and gadgets had to be bought or borrowed from friends. The one kitchen tool we used the most was a blender; we assume that almost every household has a hand blender. Also, we used a high-performance juicer – that's probably something not everyone has at home, but maybe you could borrow one.

Be sure to check the Internet if you are having problems finding the more "exotic" ingredients. Everything we used can be ordered from various websites. Of course, you can always search for alternative ingredients.

The book is written in American English, so the American weights and measurements are listed first (cups, ounces, fluid ounces, etc.) - the corresponding British terms are displayed in brackets.

We used a regular gas stove and a convection oven/fan-assisted oven. The preparation times and oven temperatures given for each recipe are only approximate and may vary, depending on what kind of stove or oven you use. Of course, it is essential to rely on your own cooking experiences. For example, if you know your oven tends to run hot, remember to cut down the cooking times.

Olive oil is a basic ingredient for our recipes. In some of the dishes the exact amount used is not mentioned, for example, if the oil is used for frying. The same goes for salt and pepper – please use these ingredients according to your own taste. You will notice that we used different types of salt and pepper, depending on the color of the menu.

Each recipe in this book serves at least four people. If you want to cook for larger groups, you can adjust the recipes accordingly. We found it best to plan the menu with more than one cook and to split the preparation of the individual courses. The effort that is necessary to obtain the ingredients needs to be taken into account, as well as the actual hands-on preparation time. Please be aware that almost every person has a different color perception. This makes no difference for colors like black or white, but may cause problems with colors like green, which can have several shades.

The experimental spirit of the menus should encourage improvisation and the use of alternative ingredients. In other words, you should feel free to use plain asparagus instead of wild asparagus and vary from our method of preparation. We used a special type of paper for the recipe pages in this book so you can jot down your own notes and ideas. In this way, *The Designer's Cookbook* will become a treasured and one-of-a-kind reference.

MENU

01

Apéritif

SALTY LASSI

Appetizer

SUMMER ROLLS

Hors d'oeuvre

PARSNIP SOUP

Drink

WHITE WINE SPRITZER

Main course

**SAUTÉED SOLE
WITH WHITE WINE SAUCE,
CAULIFLOWER RISOTTO
AND STEAMED PEARL ONIONS**

Dessert

**COCONUT PANNA COTTA
WITH MERINGUE**

Digestif

PASTIS

Appetizer

SUMMER ROLLS

---

8 round rice paper sheets

½ radish

1 parsley root

2 white beets

1 parsnip

1 or 2 hearts of romaine

3.5 oz. (100 g) glass noodles

4.4 oz. (125 g) tofu

3.5 oz. (100 g) bean sprouts

1 package enoki mushrooms

4 spring onions

8 garlic cloves

0.6 oz. (15 g) fresh ginger

½ bunch cilantro (coriander)

4 sheets parchment paper and butcher's twine

DIPPING SAUCE

6 tbsp. rice vinegar

3 tbsp. white sugar

1 organic lime

1 chili pepper

1 garlic clove

0.6 oz. (15 g) fresh ginger

1 stalk lemongrass

1 pinch salt

Pat dry the tofu with a paper towel and cut into approximately ⅓ inch wide slices. Peel the ginger and garlic and cut into fine rings along with the green leaves of the spring onions. Next, top each tofu slice with ginger, garlic and spring onion rings, add cilantro and wrap in parchment paper and secure with butcher's twine. In a saucepan, steam tofu "packages" for 7 minutes and then let cool. Remove ginger, garlic and onions and cut tofu into long, thin strips. Cook glass noodles according to package instructions using boiling salted water. Drain noodles and let cool.

Finely chop the very light, almost white part of the hearts of romaine. Slice the white part of the spring onions. Cut the remaining vegetables into fine strips. Quickly swipe a rice paper sheet through a bowl of lukewarm water and place onto a wooden board or plate. Put a little of each ingredient (vegetable strips, tofu, glass noodles, enoki mushrooms and bean sprouts) in the middle of the rice paper. Pull the bottom edge over the fillings and tuck it in on the other side, then fold in the sides and roll it up the rest of the way.

For the dipping sauce, finely grate lime zest and squeeze the juice from the lime. Combine sugar and rice vinegar in a bowl and stir until sugar dissolves, then add the lime juice. Thinly slice the lemongrass. Remove seeds from the chili pepper, press the garlic through a garlic press and grate the ginger. Next, place all (except for the white parts of the lemongrass) in a paper tea filter and add lime zest and a pinch of salt. Place filter in the rice vinegar mixture and let stand overnight. Before serving, remove tea filter and garnish the dip with the white parts of the lemongrass.

Preparation time: 1 hour + 12 hours marinating time

Hors d'oeuvre

PARSNIP SOUP

VEGETABLE STOCK

1.6 lb. (750 g) mixed white vegetables, e.g. white carrots,
cauliflower, celeriac, parsley root, white leek leaves
2 white onions
1 clove garlic
3 cloves
3 bay leaves
84 fl. oz. (2.5 l) water
Salt
Freshly ground white pepper
Sunflower oil

SOUP

1 lb. (500 g) parsnip
1 parsley root
1 white onion
6.7 fl. oz. (200 ml) heavy (double) cream
Freshly ground nutmeg
Salt
Freshly ground white pepper
Sunflower oil

For the vegetable stock, wash and dice vegetables. Chop the remaining ingredients. Heat oil in a large saucepan and briefly fry vegetables. Add 84.5 fl. oz. (2.5 l) of water and simmer for approximately 60 minutes over low heat or until liquid has reduced to 50.7 fl. oz. (1.5 l). Remove from heat and let cool for 20 minutes. Pass stock through a fine sieve and season with salt and pepper. Use immediately.

For the soup, dice parsnips. Thinly slice the parsley root and dice the white onion. Heat oil in a large saucepan. Briefly fry parsnips, onions and parsley root and add the hot vegetable stock. Bring soup to a boil, then reduce the heat and simmer for 30 minutes. Once the root vegetables are soft, remove pan from stove and finely purée the soup with a hand-held blender. Season with salt, white pepper and ground nutmeg. Next, whip cream until stiff. With a tablespoon, spoon cream into parsnip soup for a nice, fluffy consistency.

Preparation time: 3 hours

Main course

SAUTÉED SOLE
WITH WHITE WINE SAUCE,
CAULIFLOWER RISOTTO
AND STEAMED PEARL ONIONS

CAULIFLOWER RISOTTO
Cauliflower cream sauce
10.5 oz. (300 g) cauliflower
⅕ cup (50 ml) heavy (double) cream
⅕ cup (50 ml) whole milk
¼ cup (50 ml) chicken stock
Bowl ice-cold water

Risotto
8 oz. (250 g) Arborio rice
2 cups (500 ml) chicken stock
3 tbsp. (40 ml) dry white wine
3 tbsp. (40 ml) white vermouth
1 white onion
1 garlic clove
3 tsp. mascarpone
½ cup (40 g) Parmesan cheese, freshly grated
Salt
Freshly ground white pepper
Olive oil

PEARL ONIONS
20 pearl onions
Salt

For the cauliflower cream sauce, cut cauliflower into florets. Heat water in a saucepan over high heat and bring to a boil. Submerge cauliflower florets into water and blanche for 2 to 3 minutes. Remove the florets from the boiling water and immediately submerge them in a bowl of ice-cold water. Combine chicken stock, cream and milk and bring to a boil, add the blanched florets and let simmer for 30 minutes. Finally, purée sauce in a blender or food processor and pass through a fine sieve.

For the risotto, peel and finely chop onions and garlic clove. In a large saucepan, heat the oil and sauté onions and garlic until translucent. Add rice and stir until rice turns translucent. At the same time, heat the chicken stock in another saucepan. Add white wine and vermouth to the sautéed rice and simmer. Stir continuously, until all of the alcohol has evaporated. Add the stock slowly, ladleful by ladleful. Let simmer until rice is al dente, stirring frequently. When rice is almost ready, add the cauliflower cream sauce and the mascarpone and simmer for 1 to 2 minutes. Remove saucepan from stove, stir in the grated Parmesan and season with salt and white pepper.

Peel onions thoroughly. Add onions to a saucepan, cover with salted water and cook until al dente.

Preparation time: 1 hour

SAUTÉED SOLE WITH WHITE WINE SAUCE
Sole
8 to 12 (2 to 3 filets per person) sole filets
¼ cup (50 ml) fish stock
3 tbsp. (40 g) soft butter
Salt
Freshly ground white pepper
Parchment paper

Sauce
5 fl. oz. (150 ml) dry white wine
1.35 fl. oz. (40 ml) vermouth
5 fl. oz. (150 ml) fish stock
3.4 fl. oz. (100 ml) heavy (double) cream
3 tbsp. (40 g) cold butter
1 small white onion
½ cup (50 g) freshly ground horseradish
1 ½ tsp. white wine vinegar
Salt
Freshly ground white pepper

For the sauce, peel onion and cut into rings. In a saucepan, heat half of the cold butter and briefly sauté onion. Add wine and vermouth and simmer until liquid has reduced to one half, then add 5 fl. oz. (150 ml) of fish stock and cream. Add the grated horseradish and simmer, stirring occasionally, until sauce has reduced by one-third.

Preheat oven to 350 °F/180 °C/gas 4. While the sauce reduces, grease a shallow, ovenproof casserole dish with soft butter (use a brush). Thoroughly wash the sole filets and dab dry, then lightly season with salt and pepper. Fold each filet in half and place in the casserole dish. Spread the remaining soft butter on top and pour the fish stock over the filets. Cover with parchment paper and place on the middle rack. Bake for 8 to 10 minutes, checking frequently. Remove fish from the oven as soon as it has finished cooking to prevent it from drying out.

Pass the sauce through a fine sieve. Using a whisk, stir in the remaining cold butter, piece by piece. Season with white wine vinegar, salt and pepper.

Preparation time: 30 minutes

Total preparation time:
1.5 hours

Dessert

COCONUT PANNA COTTA WITH MERINGUE

PANNA COTTA
5 fl. oz. (150 ml) coconut milk
1 ¼ cup (300 ml) heavy (double) cream
⅓ cup (40 g) homemade vanilla sugar
(simply place a used vanilla bean in an airtight jar of sugar
and leave it for at least two weeks)
3 gelatin sheets
Bowl of cold water

MERINGUE (MAKES 8)
1 egg
1.7 oz. (50 g) powdered sugar
1 pinch salt
Lemon juice (just a few drops)

For the panna cotta, soak the gelatin sheets in a little cold water until soft. Mix coconut milk, cream and sugar in a saucepan, bring to a boil and simmer over low heat for 5 minutes. Remove from stove. Squeeze out any excess water from the softened gelatin sheets and then whisk them into the hot coconut cream mixture until they dissolve. Rinse four ramekins with cold water. Divide the mixture among the four ramekins and leave to cool. Cover and place in the fridge for at least 4 hours or until set.

For the meringues, preheat oven to 300°F/150°C/gas 2. Separate egg and transfer egg white to a dry metal or glass bowl. Slowly beat egg white until stiff, adding 1 pinch of salt and a few drops of lemon juice. Slowly drizzle in sugar. Beat egg white until stiff and glossy and the sugar has dissolved. Line a baking sheet with parchment paper and spoon out eight tablespoon-sized dollops of meringue. Turn the heat down to 212°F/100°C/gas ¼. If you are using a conventional oven, prop it open by placing a wooden spoon between the oven and door (if you have convection oven, this won't be necessary). Let meringues dry in the oven for about 3 to 4 hours, then remove. The meringues should still be shiny and white.

To serve, run a small knife around the edges of each ramekin, dip the bottoms into warm water and then invert onto a dessert plate. Top with crumbled meringue.

Preparation time:
35 minutes + 4 hours cooling time + 3–4 hours drying time

Apéritif

SALTY LASSI

2 cups (500 ml) low fat plain yogurt (1.5%)
6.7 fl. oz. (200 ml) whole milk
Juice of ½ a lemon
Salt to taste (e.g. sea salt)

In a blender, mix all ingredients (milk and yogurt should be cold!) until foamy. Serve immediately.

Preparation time: 5 minutes

Drink

WHITE WINE SPRITZER

1 bottle dry light white wine
1 bottle sparkling mineral water

In a jug, mix both beverages (1:1). Serve cold.

Preparation time: 5 minutes

Digestif

PASTIS

4 fl. oz. (12 cl) pastis
20.2 fl. oz. (600 ml) iced water
Ice cubes

For each drink, pour 1 fl. oz. (3 cl) of pastis into a tall glass. Fill a jug with iced water. Pour iced water over the pastis (standard 5:1 ratio) and then add ice cubes.

Preparation time: 5 minutes

INGREDIENTS

½ radish

2 white beets

1.5 lb. (700 g) parsnip

2 parsley roots

10.5 oz. (300 g) cauliflower

1 or 2 hearts of romaine

1.6 lb. (750 g) mixed white vegetables, e.g. white carrots, cauliflower, celeriac, parsley root, white leek leaves

1 package enoki mushrooms

3.5 oz. (100 g) bean sprouts

4 spring onions

20 pearl onions

5 white onions

11 garlic cloves

½ cup (50 g) freshly ground horseradish

1.2 oz. (30 g) fresh ginger

1 stalk lemongrass

1 chili pepper

½ bunch cilantro (coriander)

1 lemon

1 organic lime

Salt

Freshly ground white pepper

Freshly ground nutmeg

3 cloves

3 bay leaves

8 to 12 sole filets

1 egg

2 cups (500 ml) low fat plain yogurt (1.5%)

8.4 fl. oz. (250 ml) whole milk

22 fl. oz. (650 ml) heavy (double) cream

6 tbsp. (80 g) butter

3 tsp. mascarpone

½ cup (40 g) Parmesan cheese

4.4 oz. (125 g) tofu

6.7 fl. oz. (200 ml) fish stock

18.6 fl. oz. (550 ml) chicken stock

Olive oil

Sunflower oil

6 tbsp. rice vinegar

1 ½ tsp. white wine vinegar

5 fl. oz. (150 ml) coconut milk

8 oz. (250 g) Arborio rice

3.5 oz. (100 g) glass noodles

8 round rice paper sheets

3 tbsp. white sugar

1.7 oz. (50 g) powdered sugar

⅓ cup (40 g) homemade vanilla sugar

3 gelatin sheets

1 bottle + 6.4 fl. oz. (190 ml) dry light white wine

4 fl. oz. (12 cl) pastis

2.7 fl. oz. (80 ml) white vermouth

1 bottle sparkling mineral water

20.2 fl. oz. (600 ml) iced water

Ice cubes

Parchment paper

Butcher's twine

01

02

03

04

05

06

07

04 Main course 05 Apéritif 06 Hors d'oeuvre 07 Digestif

MENU

02

Apéritif
LICORICE LIQUEUR

Appetizer
BELUGA LENTIL SALAD

Hors d'oeuvre
MAKI SUSHI

Drink
COLA

Main course
BLACK LINGUINE WITH TAPENADE

Dessert
POPPY SEED CAKE

Digestif
ESPRESSO

Appetizer

BELUGA LENTIL SALAD

---

1 cup (200 g) black beluga lentils
¾ cup (100 g) pitted black olives (salt-marinated)
20.2 fl. oz. (600 ml) water
3 eggplants (aubergines)
1 medium-sized onion
1 pinch black cumin
2 garlic cloves
Black salt
Freshly ground black pepper
Olive oil

DRESSING
4 tbsp. balsamic vinegar
1 tbsp. honey
3 tbsp. olive oil
Black salt
Freshly ground black pepper

Wash lentils. In a saucepan, bring 20.2 fl. oz. (600 ml) of water to a boil and cook lentils over low heat for 20 minutes. Drain and season with salt.

Wash the eggplants and cut them in slices about as thick as a finger, with the skins on. Place slices cut side up on a large plate. To remove the bitter flavor, sprinkle with salt, let stand for 10 minutes, and then blot any excess water from the eggplants with a paper towel. Peel and dice onion and one clove of garlic. In a frying pan, heat some oil and briefly fry onion and cumin, then add the diced garlic and fry for a few minutes. Remove from pan. Lightly crush 3 garlic cloves. Add oil to the pan and heat. Briefly fry garlic and then remove from the pan. Next, briefly fry both sides of the eggplant slices in the garlic oil, season with salt and pepper and drain to get rid of the excess oil. Finely chop olives.

For the dressing, heat a small saucepan and bring vinegar to a boil. Simmer until the vinegar has thickened and reduced by one half. Remove from heat and stir in honey. Let cool, then mix with 3 tbsp. of oil. Season with salt and freshly ground pepper.

Mix lentils with olives, roasted onions and the dressing. Serve lentil salad with eggplant slices.

Preparation time: 1 hour

Hors d'oeuvre

MAKI SUSHI

FILLING

9.7 oz. (275 g) black radish
6 tbsp. dark soy sauce
0.5 oz. (15 g) fresh ginger
2 tbsp. rice vinegar
1 tbsp. cane (brown) sugar
1 chili pepper

SUSHI

1 cup (250 g) black sticky rice
4 nori leaves (seaweed)
12.7 fl. oz. (375 ml) water
Wasabi paste
4 tbsp. black sesame seeds

SPICED VINEGAR

3 tbsp. rice vinegar
1 tbsp. sweet rice wine
1 tsp. black salt
2 tsp. cane (brown) sugar

1 bamboo sushi rolling mat
1.7 oz. (50 g) black caviar (ice-cold)
¼ cup (50 ml) dark soy sauce

For the marinade, combine soy sauce, rice vinegar, sugar, chili pepper and grated ginger. Peel radish and cook in salt water for 30 minutes, then let cool. Cut radish in short, thin matchsticks. Add to the marinade and place in the fridge for a day, stirring occasionally.

Preparation time:
40 minutes + 1 day marinating time

Rinse rice thoroughly and repeat until water runs clear. Over medium heat, bring 12.7 fl. oz. (375 ml) of water and rice to a boil. Cover with a lid and turn down the heat to its lowest setting. Let rice simmer for about 15 minutes, then remove from heat. Allow the rice to steam for another 15 minutes.

For the spiced vinegar, heat a saucepan over low heat and mix rice vinegar, rice wine, salt and sugar. Stir until sugar has dissolved. Remove from heat and let cool.

Once the rice has finished steaming, spoon it into a flat bowl and combine with the vinegar mixture (use a wooden spoon). Let rice cool down for a few minutes until it reaches room temperature.

Place a nori sheet on your rolling mat. Wet your hands with water. Spread rice evenly (about ⅓ inch thick) over the nori by pressing with wet fingertips, leaving a 1-inch border at the far edge. Smear a small amount of wasabi onto the lower third and place marinated black radish and some sesame seeds on top of the rice. Roll up tightly with the sushi mat to form a neatly packed cylinder. Roll from bottom to top, back and forth, until it is tight. Seal it by wetting the upper end of the nori sheet with a bit of water. Repeat with the remaining nori leaves. Next, cut rolls into bite-sized pieces using a wet, sharp knife and sprinkle with lots of sesame seeds.

Serve with ice-cold caviar (do not use a silver spoon for the caviar) and a small bowl of soy sauce.

Preparation time: 1.5 hours

Total preparation time:
2 hours and 10 minutes + 1 day marinating time

Main course

BLACK LINGUINE WITH TAPENADE

1.3 lb. (600 g) fresh squid ink linguine

TAPENADE
3.5 oz. (100 g) black Gemlik olives
(salty, marinated, Turkish olives)
⅓ cup (50 g) soft, black prunes
⅓ cup (50 g) currants
½ garlic clove
1.5 tsp. sweet mustard
1 tbsp. lemon juice
3.4 fl. oz. (100 ml) water
⅓ cup (80 ml) olive oil
Black salt

In a saucepan, cover prunes and currants with 1.7 fl. oz. (50 ml) of water and let simmer for 15 minutes until soft. In the meantime, remove the pits from the olives. Combine olives with the cooked prunes and then add the currants. In a blender, purée half of the olive-prune-currant mix with 1.7 fl. oz. (50 ml) of water, peeled garlic and mustard. Dice what remains of the olive-prune-currant mix and then combine with the puréed mixture. Next, add oil and stir well. Season to taste with lemon juice and a hint of black salt.

Cook linguine in a decent amount of salted water until al dente and serve with the tapenade.

Preparation time: 30 minutes

Dessert

POPPY SEED CAKE

---

7 oz. (200 g) ground poppy seeds
¾ cup (150 g) cane (brown) sugar
⅔ cup (150 g) butter
1 tbsp. butter (to grease pan)
5 eggs
1 vanilla bean
1 organic lemon

Grease a loaf pan with butter. Wash the lime with hot water and grate the zest. Slice vanilla bean lengthwise and scrape out the seeds. Separate eggs and in one bowl, beat egg yolks and sugar until foamy. In another bowl, beat the egg whites until stiff. Melt butter, cool, and then add to the egg yolk and sugar mixture. Add poppy seeds, vanilla seeds and lemon zest. Finally, carefully fold in the stiff egg whites. Preheat oven to 338 °F/170 °C/gas 3–4 and bake for 35 minutes.

Preparation time:
20 minutes + 35 minutes baking time

Apéritif

LICORICE LIQUEUR

2.6 oz. (75 g) pure licorice
(found at organic food store or on the Internet)
17 fl. oz. (500 ml) vodka
¾ cup (150 g) cane (brown) sugar
1 tbsp. aniseed
2 star aniseed

Combine all dry ingredients in a wide-necked bottle.
Add vodka and seal. Leave in a dark place for one week,
shaking gently every once in a while, until licorice is
fully dissolved and the liqueur has turned black. Strain
the liqueur through a clean kitchen towel or coffee filter
into a clean bottle. Seal and leave in a dark, cool place
for another week.

Preparation time:
15 minutes + 2 weeks storage time

Digestif

ESPRESSO

Use a strong roast for your espresso.

Drink

COLA

At least 33.8 fl. oz. (1 l) cola
(use the darkest cola you can get)

Serve chilled.

O2

INGREDIENTS

3 eggplants (aubergines)
9.7 oz. (275 g) black radish
1 chili pepper
1 medium-sized onion
2 ½ garlic cloves
0.5 oz. (15 g) fresh ginger
1 organic lemon

1 vanilla bean
1 tbsp. aniseed
2 star aniseed
1 pinch black cumin
Black salt
Freshly ground black pepper

1.7 oz. (50 g) black caviar (ice-cold)
5 eggs

⅔ cup (150 g) butter

5.7 fl. oz. (170 ml) olive oil
1 tbsp. sweet rice wine
5 tbsp. rice vinegar
4 tbsp. balsamic vinegar
4.7 fl. oz. (140 ml) dark soy sauce
1 tbsp. honey
Wasabi paste
1.5 tsp. sweet mustard

1.3 lb. (600 g) fresh squid ink linguine
3.5 oz. (100 g) black Gemlik olives (salty, marinated, Turkish olives)
¾ cup (100 g) pitted black olives (salt-marinated)
⅓ cup (50 g) soft, black prunes
⅓ cup (50 g) currants
4 nori leaves (seaweed)

1 cup (200 g) black beluga lentils
1 cup (250 g) black sticky rice
4 tbsp. black sesame seeds
7 oz. (200 g) ground poppy seeds
11.6 oz. (330 g) cane (brown) sugar
2.6 oz. (75 g) pure licorice (found at organic food store or on the Internet)
Espresso (strong roast)

17 fl. oz. (500 ml) vodka
33.8 fl. oz. (1 l) cola (the darkest you can get)

1 bamboo sushi rolling mat

01

02

03

04

01 Apéritif 02 Main course 03 Appetizer 04 Dessert

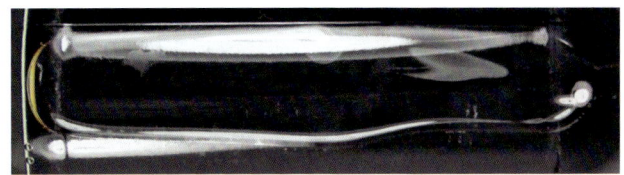

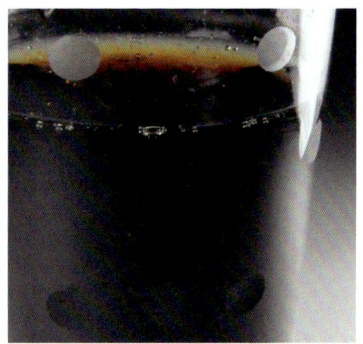

05

06

07

05 Drink   06 Hors d'oeuvre   07 Digestif

MENU

03

Apéritif

SWEET TEA WITH CREAM

Appetizer

MUSHROOM SOUP

Hors d'oeuvre

**JERUSALEM ARTICHOKE
PIZZA**

Drink

WHISKEY SOUR

Main course

**STIR-FRIED PORK STEAKS
WITH CHESTNUT SAUCE
AND BROWN RICE**

Dessert

CRÈME CARAMEL

Digestif

CAFÉ AU LAIT

Appetizer

MUSHROOM SOUP

VEGETABLE STOCK

1.3 lb. (600 g) mixed white vegetables,
e.g. celeriac, parsley root, white turnip

2 white onions

1 garlic clove

3 cloves

3 bay leaves

2.6 qt. (2.5 l) water

Salt

Freshly ground white pepper

Sunflower oil

SOUP

1 lb. (500 g) mixed mushrooms, e.g. brown and white button
mushrooms, chanterelles etc.

10 dried porcini

1 potato

2 onions

2 garlic cloves

3.4 fl. oz. (100 ml) dry sherry

5 fl. oz. (150 ml) heavy (double) cream

Salt

Freshly ground white pepper

Olive oil

1 tbsp. butter

For the stock, wash and dice vegetables and coarsely chop all remaining ingredients. In a large saucepan, heat some oil. Briefly fry the vegetables and then add 2.6 qt. (2.5 l) of water and let simmer for about 60 minutes over low heat, or until the liquid has reduced by half. Set aside for 20 minutes. Pass stock through a sieve and season with salt. Use immediately.

For the soup, soak dried porcini for 10 minutes in 6.7 fl. oz. (200 ml) of hot water. Peel potato and cut into small pieces. Wash and clean 14 oz. (400 g) of the mushrooms and cut into quarters. Peel and dice onions and garlic and fry in olive oil until translucent. Add potato and mushrooms and fry for 2 more minutes. Season with salt. Next, add the sherry and reduce until almost dry, then add the vegetable stock and the soaked porcini (including the water). Bring to a boil, cover with a lid and cook over medium heat for 20 minutes.

In the meantime, wash and slice the remaining 3.5 oz. (100 g) of mushrooms. Heat 2 tbsp. of oil and 1 tbsp. of butter in a non-stick frying pan and fry mushrooms until light brown. Season with salt and pepper.

Add the cream to the soup and season with salt and pepper. In a blender, finely purée the soup. Garnish with the fried mushrooms and serve.

Preparation time: 2 hours

Hors d'oeuvre

JERUSALEM ARTICHOKE PIZZA

DOUGH

5.2 oz. (150 g) white spelt flour
¼ cube (10 g) fresh yeast
2.7 fl. oz. (80 ml) lukewarm water
½ tbsp. white sugar
Salt

CREAM SAUCE

⅛ cup (25 g) peeled, finely ground almonds
¼ cup (25 g) macadamia nuts
½ cup (25 g) pine nuts
¼ cup (25 g) walnuts
1.7 fl. oz. (50 ml) water
1 tbsp. lemon juice
Salt

TOPPING

8 oz. (250 g) Jerusalem artichoke
4 tbsp. almond oil
1 garlic clove
Salt
Freshly ground white pepper
2 tbsp. (20 g) sesame seeds

For the dough, sift the flour into a bowl. Make a well in the center, crumble in the yeast and add ½ tbsp. of sugar and 2 tbsp. of lukewarm water, then lightly dust with flour. Cover bowl with a kitchen towel and leave to rise for 20 minutes in a warm place. Next, add 2.7 fl. oz. (80 ml) of lukewarm water to the dough and season with salt. Knead well, cover with a towel and let rise in a warm place for 30 more minutes.

Meanwhile, add all of the ingredients for the cream sauce to a blender and blend until smooth. Peel garlic cloves and press through a garlic press. Mix with almond oil and allow to infuse. Peel and finely slice Jerusalem artichoke (you might want to use a grater).

Preheat oven to 350 °F/180 °C/gas 4. After the dough has risen, knead well and dust with flour to prevent the dough from sticking. Cut into 4 equal pieces and on a flour-dusted workspace, roll out each piece until it is very thin. Place on a baking tray lined with parchment paper. Spread some of the almond nut cream and almond oil on to each piece. Top with a layer of Jerusalem artichoke, brush with the rest of the almond oil and sprinkle with sesame seeds. Season with salt and pepper and bake for 12 to 15 minutes on the middle rack.

Preparation time:
50 minutes + 50 minutes rising time

Main course

STIR-FRIED PORK STEAKS WITH CHESTNUT SAUCE AND BROWN RICE

Pork loin steaks or pork medallions,
4.4 oz. (125 g) per person

SAUCE
8 oz. (250 g) cooked chestnuts
1.3 fl. oz. (40 ml) cognac
1.3 fl. oz. (40 ml) heavy (double) cream
2 tbsp. butter
2.5 fl. oz. (75 ml) water
Salt
Freshly ground white pepper
Clarified butter
Olive oil

RICE
1 cup (200 g) brown rice
1 small onion
Freshly ground nutmeg
13.5 fl. oz. (400 ml) water
Salt
Olive oil

For the rice, peel and dice the onion. Heat some olive oil and fry onion until translucent. Add nutmeg and rice and simmer for 2 more minutes. Next, add 13.5 fl. oz. (400 ml) of water, bring to a boil and simmer for approximately 40 minutes over low heat or until the rice is done. Season with salt and cover to keep warm.

In a blender, purée 5.2 oz. (150 g) of chestnuts, 1 tbsp. of olive oil and 2.6 fl. oz. (75 ml) of water. Cut the remaining chestnuts in half and set aside. Heat some clarified butter in a frying pan and brown pork steaks for about 3 to 4 minutes on each side. Wrap steaks in aluminum foil and set aside. Next, heat some butter in the same pan and fry the chestnut halves. Add cognac, chestnut purée and cream and simmer for 5 minutes over low heat. Season with salt and pepper. Pour a bit of the chestnut sauce onto prepared plates, add the pork steaks and serve with the rice and chestnut halves.

Preparation time: 1.5 hours

03

Dessert

CRÈME CARAMEL

––––––––––––––––––––––––––––

1 cup (250 ml) almond milk
1 cup (250 ml) heavy (double) cream
3.5 oz. white sugar
2 tbsp. (20 g) cane (brown) sugar
1.7 fl. oz. (50 ml) warm water
4 eggs
1 vanilla bean
Butter

4 soufflé dishes (Ø 3.1 inches / 8 cm)

Lightly grease 4 soufflé dishes with butter. In a saucepan, melt 3.5 oz. (100 g) of sugar over medium heat until golden brown. Carefully add 1.7 fl. oz. (50 ml) of warm water. Simmer over low heat, stirring constantly, until caramel melts into liquid. Immediately pour the liquid into the soufflé dishes and shake them gently to evenly coat the bottoms and sides. Place the dishes in the fridge for 30 minutes.

Slice 1 vanilla bean lengthwise and scrape out the seeds. In a saucepan, heat 1 cup (250 ml) of almond milk, 1 cup (250 ml) of heavy cream, 2 tbsp. of cane sugar and then the vanilla bean and seeds. Bring to a boil, remove from heat and let cool for 10 minutes. Remove vanilla bean.

Separate two eggs and beat the egg yolks with 2 whole eggs. Combine the milk mixture with the egg mixture and pour into the caramel coated soufflé dishes. Next, place the four small dishes into a large casserole dish and add about 1 inch of boiling water. Place in a preheated oven and bake at 350 °F/180 °C/gas 4 on bottom rack for 40 minutes (it is not recommended to use a convection oven for this step!). To prevent the top from burning, cover with aluminum foil. After baking, remove from oven and let cool. Place soufflés in the fridge for 2 hours, then run a sharp knife around the inside of each dish and invert on to dessert plates.

Preparation time: 1 hour + 2.5 hours cooling time

Digestif

CAFÉ AU LAIT

Espresso
13.5 fl. oz. (400 ml) whole milk

Use a light espresso roast for the coffee. For each glass,
combine coffee with 3.4 fl. oz. (100 ml) of hot milk.

Preparation time: 10 minutes

Apéritif

SWEET TEA WITH CREAM

Rich black tea blend
33.8 fl. oz. (1 l) water
⅓ cup (80 ml) heavy (double) cream
Brown rock candy (rock sugar)

Add 5 tsp. of the black tea to a tea filter and then add
33.8 fl. oz. (1 l) of boiling water and let stand for 3 minutes. Add cream and sweeten with rock candy.

Preparation time: 10 minutes

Drink

WHISKEY SOUR

5.4 fl. oz. (16 cl) Bourbon whiskey
2 fl. oz. (6 cl) lime juice (approx. 2 limes)
⅓ cup (60 g) cane (brown) sugar
2 fl. oz. (60 ml) water
Ice cubes

Squeeze limes. In a small saucepan, bring ⅓ cup (60 g)
of cane sugar and 2 fl. oz. (60 ml) of water to a boil,
stirring constantly until the sugar has dissolved. Let cool.
For each cocktail, add 1.3 fl. oz. (4 cl) of whiskey, 0.5 fl. oz.
(1.5 cl) of lime juice, 0.5 fl. oz. (1.5 cl) of sugar syrup
and 3 ice cubes to a cocktail shaker and shake for
10 seconds. Strain into a whiskey sour glass and serve.

Preparation time: 30 minutes

INGREDIENTS

1 lb. (500 g) mixed mushrooms,
e.g. brown and white button mushrooms, chanterelles etc.
8 oz. (250 g) cooked chestnuts
8 oz. (250 g) Jerusalem artichoke
1.3 lb. (600 g) mixed white vegetables, e.g. celeriac,
parsley root, white turnip
1 potato
3 onions
2 white onions
4 garlic cloves

2 limes
1 tbsp. lemon juice

1 vanilla bean
3 cloves
3 bay leaves
Freshly ground nutmeg
Salt
Freshly ground white pepper

17.6 oz. (500 g) pork loin steaks or pork medallions
4 eggs

13.5 fl. oz. (400 ml) whole milk
8.4 fl. oz. (250 ml) heavy (double) cream
4 tbsp. butter
Clarified butter

Sunflower oil
Olive oil
4 tbsp. almond oil

5.2 oz. (150 g) white spelt flour
1 cup (200 g) brown rice
10 dried porcini
1/8 cup (25 g) peeled, finely ground almonds
1/4 cup (25 g) macadamia nuts
1/2 cup (25 g) pine nuts
1/4 cup (25 g) walnuts
2 tbsp. (20 g) sesame seeds
Espresso, light roast
Rich black tea blend
3.5 oz. (100 g) white sugar
2.8 oz. (80 g) cane (brown) sugar
Brown rock candy (rock sugar)
1/4 cube (10 g) fresh yeast

1 cup (250 ml) almond milk
3.4 fl. oz. (100 ml) dry sherry
5.4 fl. oz. (16 cl) Bourbon whiskey
1.3 fl. oz. (40 ml) cognac

Ice cubes

4 soufflé dishes (Ø 3.1 inches / 8 cm)

01

02

03

01 Appetizer 02 Drink 03 Main course

04

05

06

07

MENU

04

Apéritif

KIWI LIME PUNCH

Appetizer

CHILLED AVOCADO SOUP

Hors d'oeuvre

GREEN ASPARAGUS SALAD

Drink

GREEN GRAPE LEMONADE

Main course

**CHICKEN BREAST WITH
OLIVE PESTO AND ZUCCHINI
(COURGETTE) CARPACCIO**

Dessert

**GREEN TEA ICE CREAM
WITH PISTACHIO COOKIES**

Digestif

TRIPLE GREEN MOJITO

Appetizer

CHILLED AVOCADO SOUP

VEGETABLE STOCK
1 lb. (500 g) mixed green and white vegetables,
e.g. celery, leek, zucchini (courgette), parsnip
2 white onions
1 garlic clove
3 cloves
3 bay leaves
50.7 fl. oz. (1.5 l) water
Salt
Freshly ground white pepper
Olive oil

SOUP
2 avocados
2 small cucumbers
5 spring onions
1 lime
1 bunch cilantro (coriander)
1 garlic clove
1 tsp. green Tabasco
Salt
Freshly ground green pepper
1 tbsp. olive oil

For the vegetable stock, wash and dice the vegetables. Coarsely chop the remaining ingredients. In a large saucepan, heat oil and add vegetables. Briefly fry, then add 50.7 fl. oz. (1.5 l) of water and simmer over low heat for about 50 minutes or until the liquid has reduced by one half. Remove from heat for 20 minutes. Pass stock through a fine sieve and season with salt. Use stock immediately.

Cut avocado in half, remove pit and skin and cut into eighths. Peel cucumber, cut in half and remove seeds with a spoon. Cut spring onions into fine rings. Squeeze lime juice, remove cilantro leaves from the stalks and purée in a blender with garlic clove and 1 tbsp. of oil. Mix with vegetable stock and season with salt, pepper and Tabasco. Refrigerate for at least 2 hours.

Preparation time: 2 hours + 2 hours cooling time

Hors d'oeuvre

GREEN ASPARAGUS SALAD

---

14 oz. (400 g) wild asparagus
6 spring onions
1 small handful of green grapes (seedless)
½ lime
½ fresh light green chili pepper
4 tbsp. rice wine
2 tsp. rice vinegar
1 ½ tsp. rapeseed (canola) honey
1.1 oz. (30 g) ginger
Salt
Olive oil

Wash the wild asparagus, then wash lime with hot water and zest one half. Squeeze ½ of the lime and mix juice with lime zest, rice wine, vinegar and honey. Purée grapes in a blender and add to the sauce. Cut spring onions into thin rings. Dice the ginger and the chili pepper. In a large frying pan, heat oil and fry onions, ginger and pepper until translucent. Reduce heat to medium and add the asparagus. Simmer for 2 to 3 minutes and then add the sauce mixture. Bring to a boil and simmer for 3 more minutes. The asparagus should be tender, but still have a crunch. Season with salt. Serve asparagus with the sauce.

Preparation time: 30 minutes

Main course

CHICKEN BREAST WITH OLIVE PESTO AND ZUCCHINI (COURGETTE) CARPACCIO

4 chicken breasts
3 tbsp. butter
Salt
Freshly ground white pepper

PESTO
¾ cup (100 g) pitted green olives
1 cup (100 g) pistachios
2.5 fl. oz. (75 ml) dry white wine
1 ½ tbsp. lemon juice
3 tbsp. white balsamic vinegar
½ cup (125 ml) olive oil

CARPACCIO
4 small zucchini (courgettes)
2 ½ tbsp. white balsamic vinegar
6 tbsp. olive oil
½ cup (50 g) grated Parmesan cheese
3 garlic cloves
Salt
Freshly ground white pepper

For the pesto, mix vinegar, lemon juice and white wine and then add olive oil. Next, add finely chopped olives and pistachios and allow to marinate for at least 2 hours.

For the carpaccio, preheat oven to 400 °F/ 200 °C/gas 6. Cut zucchini into paper-thin slices and place on a baking tray. Season with a bit of salt and drizzle with olive oil. Roast for 15 to 20 minutes or until the zucchini start to brown. Remove from oven and let cool.
Meanwhile, create a marinade by combining oil, vinegar, pressed garlic and Parmesan cheese. Season with salt and pepper and allow to infuse. Add the the zucchini slices and turn them several times until they are evenly coated.

Season chicken breasts with salt and pepper and fry in butter over low heat for about 3 to 4 minutes until golden brown. Let cool. To serve, cut each breast diagonally into pieces and serve with the olive pesto and marinated zucchini.

Preparation time: 50 minutes
+ 20 minutes baking time + 2 hours cooling time

Dessert

GREEN TEA ICE CREAM WITH PISTACHIO COOKIES

ICE CREAM

0.35 oz. (10 g) matcha green tea powder
(Japanese tea powder)
1 cup (250 ml) heavy (double) cream
1 cup (250 ml) whole milk
2.8 oz. (80 g) fine white sugar
1 pinch salt

Ice cream maker or ice cubes plus 7 oz. (200 g) salt

COOKIES

1 cup (100 g) pistachios
¾ cup (90 g) cake flour (plain flour)
⅓ cup (75 g) fine white sugar
½ tsp. baking powder
1.8 oz. (50 g) soft butter
1.3 fl. oz. (40 ml) milk

For the ice cream, add all ingredients to a mixing bowl and whisk until sugar and tea have dissolved. Add mixture to an ice cream maker or you can make the ice cream in two bowls. Use one small metal bowl and one larger plastic bowl. Place the metal bowl in the plastic bowl and fill the space between the bowls with ice cubes, 8 oz. (200 g) of salt and ice cold water. Next, add the ice cream mixture to the metal bowl. Stir until ice cream hardens. Continue to scrape the ice off the sides of the bowl and stir into the mass. Place in the freezer for 8 hours, removing every once in a while to stir. The finished texture should be smooth.

Carefully roast pistachios in a frying pan (no oil!) and let cool. Next, add half of the pistachios to a blender and grind to a fine green flour. Chop the remaining nuts. Preheat oven to 350 °F/180 °C/gas 4. Combine flour and baking powder. In a bowl, mix soft butter and milk and then add the flour and mix well. Finally, add the pistachios. Line a baking tray with parchment paper and place little cookie dough portions on the baking tray. Bake for 12 minutes on the middle rack.

After approximately 8 hours in the freezer, serve 1 to 2 scoops of ice cream per person. Arrange in a dessert bowl and serve with the pistachio cookies.

Preparation time: 1 hour + 15 minutes baking time
+ 8 hours freezing time

Apéritif

KIWI LIME PUNCH

4 kiwis
3 organic limes
3.4 fl. oz. (100 ml) elderflower syrup
1 bottle Prosecco
Ice cubes

Peel kiwis and cut into small pieces. Wash one lime with hot water and grate the zest, then juice all of the limes. Mix elderflower syrup, kiwis, lime juice and lime zest and allow to stand for 30 minutes. Pour into 4 glasses and then add ice cubes and cold Prosecco.

Preparation time:
20 minutes plus 30 minutes infusing time

Drink

GREEN GRAPE LEMONADE

2.2 lb (1 kg) green seedless grapes
4 limes
1 tsp. lemon juice
1 bunch lemon balm
50.7 fl. oz. (1.5 l) sparkling mineral water

Peel limes. In a blender, purée grapes, limes, lemon juice and lemon balm and drain through a sieve into a large pitcher. Add the cold mineral water and serve immediately (to prevent lemonade from turning brown).

Preparation time: 20 minutes

Digestif

TRIPLE GREEN MOJITO

4.7 fl. oz. (14 cl) white rum
4 organic limes
2/3 cup (100 g) cucumber
9.4 fl. oz. (28 cl) still mineral water
2/3 cups (80 g) sugar
2.7 fl. oz. (80 ml) water
2 sprigs fresh mint
Ice cubes

For the syrup, heat 2/3 cup (80 g) of sugar and 2.7 oz. (80 ml) of water in a small saucepan and bring to a boil. Stir constantly until the sugar has dissolved, then remove from heat and let cool. Remove the mint leaves from the stalks. Peel cucumber and cut 1/8 cup (20 g) into slices. Slice one of the limes and juice the remaining three. In a blender, purée 1/2 cup (80 g) of cucumber and mint leaves.

For each cocktail, add 0.7 fl. oz. (2 cl) of lime juice, 0.7 fl. oz. (2 cl) of syrup and 1 tsp. of cucumber purée to a glass. Add 1.2 fl. oz. (3.5 cl) of rum, 3 ice cubes, 2 lime slices and 2 cucumber slices, then add the mineral water and stir.

Preparation time: 30 minutes

04

INGREDIENTS

3 small cucumbers

4 small zucchini (courgettes)

1 lb. (500 g) mixed green and white vegetables, e.g. celery, leek, zucchini (courgette), parsnip

2 avocados

14 oz. (400 g) wild asparagus

½ fresh light green chili pepper

11 spring onions

2 white onions

5 garlic cloves

1 bunch cilantro (coriander)

1 bunch lemon balm

2 sprigs fresh mint

1.1 oz. (30 g) ginger

2.4 lb. (1.1 kg) green seedless grapes

4 kiwis

13 organic limes

1 lemon

3 cloves

3 bay leaves

7 oz. (200 g) salt

Freshly ground white pepper

Freshly ground green pepper

4 chicken breasts

9.8 fl. oz. (290 ml) whole milk

1 cup (250 ml) heavy (double) cream

3.1 oz. (90 g) butter

½ cup (50 g) grated Parmesan cheese

8.9 fl. oz. (265 ml) olive oil

5 ½ tbsp. white balsamic vinegar

4 tbsp. rice wine

2 tsp. rice vinegar

1 ½ tsp. rapeseed (canola) honey

3.4 fl. oz. (100 ml) elderflower syrup

1 tsp. green Tabasco

¾ cup (100 g) pitted green olives

2 cups (200 g) pistachios

¾ cup (90 g) cake flour (plain flour)

½ tsp. baking powder

8.2 oz. (235 g) fine white sugar

0.35 oz. (10 g) matcha green tea powder (Japanese tea powder)

2.5 fl. oz. (75 ml) dry white wine

4.7 fl. oz. (14 cl) white rum

1 bottle Prosecco

50.7 fl. oz. (1.5 l) sparkling mineral water

9.4 fl. oz. (28 cl) still mineral water

Ice cubes

Ice cream maker or ice cubes

01

02

03

01 Hors d'oeuvre 02 Dessert 03 Main course

04

05

06

07

04 Appetizer 05 Apéritif 06 Digestif 07 Drink

MENU

05

Apéritif

MANGO LASSI

Appetizer

**TORTILLA ESPANOLA
WITH MOJO AMARILLO**

Hors d'oeuvre

YELLOW LENTIL SOUP

Drink

GINGER LEMONADE

Main course

**RAVIOLI WITH BELL PEPPER
AND RICOTTA FILLING
AND LEMON BUTTER SAUCE**

Dessert

LEMON TART

Digestif

MAI TAI

Appetizer

TORTILLA ESPANOLA
WITH MOJO AMARILLO

TORTILLA

1.5 lb (700 g) waxy yellow potatoes (e.g. Yukon Gold)
2 yellow bell peppers
3 large onions
3 eggs
Salt
Freshly ground white pepper
1/4 tsp. turmeric
Olive oil

Peel onions and cut into fine rings. Wash bell peppers and remove seeds and cut into thin slices. Peel and finely slice potatoes. In a non-stick frying pan (9.4 inches/ 24 cm), heat olive oil and fry potatoes for 20 minutes. Meanwhile, heat some olive oil in a second frying pan and sauté onions until translucent. Remove from heat. Next, fry bell peppers in olive oil until tender. Separate one egg. In a large bowl, beat egg yolk with the remaining two eggs. Season with salt and pepper and add turmeric. Add potatoes, onions and bell peppers to the eggs, mix well and let stand for 15 minutes. Heat olive oil in a non-stick frying pan, add the batter and cook over medium heat for about 10 minutes. Allow the tortilla to cook around the edges, and then carefully lift up one side of the tortilla to check if it has browned slightly. Place a large dinner plate upside down over the frying pan and quickly turn the pan over so the tortilla will "fall" onto the plate. Again, add some oil to the pan. Now slide the tortilla back into the frying pan. Cook the tortilla until done and slightly brown all over, then remove from the pan and let cool. Cut into 1 inch pieces and serve with the yellow side up.

Preparation time:
1 hour + 15 minutes standing time

MOJO

1 large yellow bell pepper
1 garlic clove
1 yellow chili pepper
1 tbsp. ground almonds
3 tbsp. orange juice
2 tbsp. white wine vinegar
2/3 cup (160 ml) olive oil
Salt
Freshly ground white pepper

Preheat oven to 425 °F/220 °C/gas 7. Wash bell pepper, remove seeds and cut into quarters. Place bell peppers skin side up in a casserole dish and bake in a preheated oven for approximately 30 minutes, or until the skin turns light brown and blisters. Remove from oven and cover with a damp paper towel until cool. Next, using a knife, remove the skins from the peppers. In a blender, purée bell peppers with the other ingredients and season with salt and pepper.

Preparation time:
15 minutes + 30 minutes baking time

Total preparation time: 75 minutes
+ 30 minutes baking time + 15 minutes standing time

Hors d'oeuvre

YELLOW LENTIL SOUP

VEGETABLE STOCK
1.3 lb. (600 g) yellow and white vegetables, e.g. yellow bell
pepper, white turnip, celeriac, parsley root, potato
2 white onions
3 cloves
3 bay leaves
2.7 qt. (2.5 l) water
Freshly ground white pepper
Sunflower oil

SOUP
1 ¾ cup (350 g) yellow lentils
2 small yellow potatoes
1 small parsnip
1 slice pineapple
0.7 oz. (20 g) fresh ginger
2 onions
1 garlic clove
1 yellow chili pepper
1 tsp. turmeric
½ tsp. ground cumin
Salt
Freshly ground white pepper
Sunflower oil

For the stock, wash and dice vegetables. Chop the remaining ingredients. Heat oil in a large saucepan and add the vegetables and spices. Briefly fry and then add 2.7 qt. (2.5 l) of water and let simmer over low heat for approximately 60 minutes, or until liquid has reduced by one half. Remove from heat and let cool for 20 more minutes, then pass stock through a fine sieve. Season with pepper. Use stock immediately.

For the soup, peel and finely chop the potatoes and parsnip. Remove seeds from the chili pepper. Peel and dice the onions and garlic and fry in oil. Dust with turmeric and cumin. Next, add the chopped vegetables and the thoroughly washed lentils and fry for 3 more minutes. Add the vegetable stock and bring to a boil. Peel and finely grate ginger and add to the soup, then add the chopped pineapple slice. Cover the saucepan loosely with a lid. Let simmer for 45 minutes over medium heat, then purée in a blender and season with salt and pepper.

Preparation time: 2 hours

Main course

RAVIOLI WITH BELL PEPPER AND RICOTTA FILLING AND LEMON BUTTER SAUCE

PASTA DOUGH
14 oz. (400 g) pastry flour
5 eggs
1 tbsp. milk
4 tbsp. olive oil
1 tsp. turmeric
1 organic lemon
¼ tsp. salt

FILLING
2 small yellow bell peppers
8 oz. (250 g) ricotta cheese
⅜ cup (50 g) pine nuts
1 pinch ground chili
Salt

LEMON BUTTER
2 organic lemons
Lemon juice
4.4 oz. (125 g) butter
2 scallions
4 tsp. olive oil
½ tsp. saffron strings
¼ tsp. turmeric
Salt

¾ cup (75 g) Parmesan cheese

Flour
Pasta machine
Pastry wheel

For the pasta dough, wash lemon with hot water and grate the zest. Combine flour, 4 eggs, oil, spices and lemon zest and knead until a smooth, stretchy dough has formed (depending on the size of the eggs, you might have to add more flour or oil). You can use either a food processor or knead the dough with your hands. Shape into a ball, wrap in plastic wrap and chill in the fridge for 30 minutes.

In the meantime, prepare the filling. Roast pine nuts in a frying pan (no oil!) until golden brown and then chop them into small pieces. Preheat oven to 425 °F/ 220 °C/ gas 7. Wash bell peppers, remove the seeds and cut into eighths. Place bell peppers skin side up on a baking tray and bake in a preheated oven on a middle rack, for approximately 25 minutes, or until the skins turns lightly brown and blister. Remove from oven and cover with a damp paper towel. Once cool, using a knife, remove skins from the peppers. In a blender, purée one bell pepper and cut the other one into small pieces. Mix with pine nuts and spices. Turn ricotta onto a clean kitchen towel and drain the liquid, then add to the bell pepper mixture.

Cut the cold dough into halves. Knead both parts and roll out flat on a workspace dusted with flour to prevent the dough from sticking. Cut dough into thin strips. Turn pasta machine to widest setting and run the dough through several times until smooth and velvety, folding before each run and dusting with flour if sticky. Adjust the machine to the next setting. Repeat, narrowing rollers after each run until the pasta is paper thin, dusting with flour if necessary. Cut the long dough pieces so they will be easier to run through the machine. On one half of the dough, use a pastry wheel to mark several squares (2.3 inches x 2.3 inches each), but do not cut through the dough. Place a bit of the filling in the center of each square.

Separate one egg and spread egg yolk onto the edges of each square. Next, cover loosely with second dough sheet. Press down around the filling to seal. Cut the ravioli with the pastry wheel and place on a clean kitchen towel dusted with flour to prevent them from sticking.

For the lemon butter, wash lemon with hot water and grate the zest. Add saffron strings to a cup with 1 ½ tsp. of boiling water and let cool for 10 minutes. Heat a small piece of butter in a frying pan and cook the coarsely chopped scallions until translucent, then add turmeric, saffron water, lemon zest and a bit of lemon juice. Melt the remaining butter, add all ingredients and toss. Season with salt.

Heat a decent amount of salted water with 1 tbsp. of oil and bring to a boil. Add ravioli and cook for 3 minutes over medium heat. With a slotted spoon, carefully remove ravioli and place on plates. Remove lemon zest, saffron and scallions from the lemon butter and pour over ravioli. Sprinkle with grated Parmesan cheese and serve.

Preparation time: 3 hours
+ 30 minutes cooling time + 30 minutes baking time

Dessert

LEMON TART

DOUGH
7.9 oz. (225 g) all-purpose flour
⅔ cup (150 g) butter
1.7 oz. (50 g) sugar
1 pinch salt

1 lb. (500 g) baking beans

TOPPING
2 organic lemons
4.4 oz. (125 g) sugar
1.7 fl. oz. (50 ml) heavy (double) cream
3 eggs

For the dough, dice the butter and combine with the remaining ingredients. Knead into a dough. Wrap in plastic wrap and chill in the fridge for 30 minutes. Dust a piece of parchment paper with flour and roll out dough until it is paper-thin. Grease a tart pan (pie dish, approx. 10 inch/27 cm). Carefully place the dough in the prepared tart pan and, using your fingertips, evenly press the pastry onto the bottom and up the sides. Preheat oven to 350 °F/180 °C/gas 4. Pierce the bottom of the crust with a fork, line with parchment paper and place baking beans on top. Bake for 25 minutes.

In the meantime, prepare the filling. Wash lemons with hot water and finely grate the zest, then squeeze lemons. In a bowl, mix the eggs, sugar, cream, 7 tablespoons (100 ml) of lemon juice and the lemon zest. Pour the lemon cream into the baked crust and bake at 250 °F/ 130 °C/gas 1–2 for an additional 30 minutes. Allow to cool and serve.

Preparation time:
45 minutes + 55 minutes baking time

Apéritif

MANGO LASSI

---

2 ripe mangos
17 fl. oz. (500 ml) plain, low-fat yogurt (1.5%)
6.7 fl. oz. (200 ml) whole milk
6.7 fl. oz. (200 ml) still mineral water

Remove pits from mangos, peel and cut into pieces. In a blender, add mangos, cold yogurt, milk and mineral water and blend until foamy. Serve immediately.

Preparation time: 10 minutes

Drink

GINGER LEMONADE

4.2 oz. (120 g) fresh ginger
½ cup lemon juice (2 to 3 lemons)
5 tbsp. honey
¼ tsp. saffron strings
2 pinches salt
50.7 fl. oz. (1.5 l) still mineral water

Squeeze lemons. In a jug, combine lemon juice with salt and 8.4 fl. oz. (250 ml) of mineral water. Peel and finely grate ginger. Add ginger purée and saffron strings with 17 fl. oz. (500 ml) of water to a saucepan and bring to a boil. Simmer for 20 minutes, then let cool. Strain through a fine sieve and add to the lemon mixture. Stir in the honey until it is fully dissolved and add the remaining mineral water. Refrigerate for 2 hours.

Preparation time:
30 minutes + 2 hours cooling time

Digestif

MAI TAI

3.4 fl. oz. (10 cl) white rum
2 fl. oz. (6 cl) brown rum
2 fl. oz. (6 cl) triple sec
3.4 fl. oz. (10 cl) lemon juice (2 to 3 lemons)
2.7 fl. oz. (8 cl) orange juice
2.7 fl. oz. (8 cl) pineapple juice
2.8 oz. (80 g) sugar
Crushed ice

Squeeze lemons and set aside 4 tsp. (2 cl) of lemon juice. In a small saucepan, mix 2.7 fl. oz. (8 cl) of lemon juice with 2.8 oz. (80 g) of sugar and bring to a boil, stirring until sugar has fully dissolved. Let cool. For each cocktail, add 5 tsp. (2.5 cl) of white rum, 1 tbsp. (1.5 cl) of brown rum, 1 tbsp. (1.5 cl) of triple sec, 4 tsp. (2 cl) of lemon syrup, 1 tsp. (0.5 cl) of lemon juice, 4 tsp. (2 cl) of orange juice, 4 tsp. (2 cl) of pineapple juice and 3 ice cubes in a cocktail shaker and shake for 10 seconds. Strain and pour into a cocktail glass and serve.

Preparation time: 30 minutes

INGREDIENTS

1.5 lb (700 g) waxy yellow potatoes (e.g. Yukon Gold)
1.3 lb. (600 g) yellow and white vegetables, e.g. yellow bell
pepper, white turnip, celeriac, parsley root, potato
2 small yellow potatoes
1 small parsnip
5 yellow bell peppers
2 yellow chili peppers
2 onions
3 large onions
2 white oninons
2 scallions
3 garlic cloves

2 ripe mangos
1 slice pineapple
4.9 oz. (140 g) fresh ginger
11 organic lemons

3 cloves
3 bay leaves
1 tsp. saffron strings
2 ½ tsp. turmeric
½ tsp. ground cumin
1 pinch ground chili
Salt
Freshly ground white pepper

11 eggs

17 fl. oz. (500 ml) plain, low-fat yogurt (1.5%)
7.4 fl. oz. (220 ml) whole milk
1.7 fl. oz. (50 ml) heavy (double) cream
8 oz. (250 g) ricotta cheese
¾ cup (75) g Parmesan cheese
9.7 oz. (275 g) butter

7.4 oz. (220 ml) olive oil
Sunflower oil
2 tbsp. white wine vinegar
5 tbsp. honey

14 oz. (400 g) pastry flour
7.9 oz. (225 g) all-purpose flour
1 ¾ cup (350 g) yellow lentils
1 lb. (500 g) baking beans
9 oz. (255 g) sugar
⅜ cup (50 g) pine nuts
1 tbsp. ground almonds

3.4 fl. oz. (10 cl) white rum
2 fl. oz. (6 cl) brown rum
2 fl. oz. (6 cl) triple sec
57.4 fl. oz. (1.7 l) still mineral water

2.7 fl. oz. (8 cl) orange juice
2.7 fl. oz. (8 cl) pineapple juice

Crushed Ice
Pasta machine
Pastry wheel

01

02

03

04

05

06

07

04 Main course   05 Dessert   06 Digestif   07 Apéritif

MENU

06

Apéritif

STRAWBERRY PUNCH

Appetizer

MELON SOUP

Hors d'oeuvre

**SERRANO AND
STRAWBERRY CARPACCIO
WITH FIG SAUCE**

Drink

RHUBARB SPRITZER

Main course

**SALMON FILET WITH
PINK HORSERADISH CRUST AND
RED BEET (BEETROOT) RISOTTO WITH
PRAWNS AND RHUBARB RELISH**

Dessert

**STRAWBERRY
AND CREAM SWISS ROLL**

Digestif

ROSÉ WINE

Appetizer

MELON SOUP

5.5 lb. (2.5 kg) watermelon
¼ cantaloupe
0.9 oz. (25 g) fresh ginger
¼ cup (20 g) sliced almonds
1 ½ limes
2.7 fl. oz. (80 ml) heavy (double) cream
Pink salt
Freshly ground pink pepper
and some whole pink peppercorns
1 pinch sugar

Heat a frying pan (without oil) on the stove and roast the almonds until they turn light brown. Cut melons in half, then into quarters and remove the seeds. Remove the rind and cut flesh into small cubes. Peel and coarsely chop the ginger. In a blender, add melon cubes, ginger and cream and blend well. Season with lime juice, salt, pepper and sugar. Garnish with some pink peppercorns.

Preparation time: 30 minutes

Hors d'oeuvre

SERRANO AND STRAWBERRY CARPACCIO WITH FIG SAUCE

8 slices serrano ham
8.8 oz. (250 g) fresh strawberries

SAUCE
4 strawberries
3 fresh figs
1 ½ tsp. acacia honey
2 tbsp. olive oil
1 tsp. white balsamic vinegar
½ tsp. Balsamico di Modena
1–2 tbsp. red grape juice
Pink salt
Freshly ground white pepper
Lemon juice

For the sauce, thoroughly wash figs and 4 strawberries. Dice the figs, then remove the stems and caps from the strawberries and combine in a blender with honey, oil, vinegar and grape juice. Blend until smooth and season with salt, pepper and lemon juice. Wash and hull the remaining strawberries, and cut into fine slices. Arrange with the serrano ham on plates, drizzle the fig sauce over the carpaccio and serve.

Preparation time: 20 minutes

Main course

SALMON FILET WITH PINK HORSERADISH CRUST AND RED BEET (BEETROOT) RISOTTO WITH PRAWNS AND RHUBARB RELISH

RHUBARB RELISH

1 small onion
10.5 oz. (300 g) rhubarb
0.7 oz. (20 g) fresh ginger
1 ½ garlic cloves
½ red chili pepper
½ cup (100 g) cane (brown) sugar
1 tsp. pink salt
Freshly ground white pepper
Sunflower oil

Peel onion and cut into ⅓ inch cubes. Thoroughly wash rhubarb. Use only the pink parts and cut them into pieces, about 0.75 inch to 1.5 inches. Next, slice the chili lengthwise, remove seeds and chop into small pieces. In a saucepan, heat oil and add onions, garlic and ginger. Sauté until translucent. Add rhubarb, chili and sugar and let simmer over low heat for 2 minutes, until rhubarb is tender but not mushy. Season with salt, pepper and add a bit of sugar if you like, then immediately pour into a clean canning jar. Close the lid and let cool.

Preparation time: 30 minutes

RED BEET (BEETROOT) RISOTTO
Vegetable stock
1 lb. (500 g) mixed vegetables,
e.g. red carrots, celeriac, parsley root
1 red onion
1 garlic clove
2 cloves
2 bay leaves
50.7 fl. oz. (1.5 l) water
Pink salt
Freshly ground white pepper
Olive oil

Risotto
10.5 oz. (300 g) Arborio rice
1 small fresh red beet (beetroot)
1 small red onion
2 sprigs rosemary
6.7 fl. oz. (200 ml) dry rosé wine
Butter
1 cup (100 g) ground Parmesan cheese
Pink salt
Freshly ground white pepper
Olive oil

For the vegetable stock, thoroughly wash and dice vegetables. Chop all the other ingredients. In a large saucepan, heat olive oil and add the vegetables. Sauté briefly, then add 50.7 fl. oz. (1.5 l) of water and let simmer until liquid has reduced to ⅓. Remove from heat and let cool for 20 minutes. Strain stock through a fine sieve and season with salt. Use stock for the risotto.

For the risotto, peel and finely chop the beet, then peel and dice the onion. In a large saucepan, heat the oil and sauté beet, onions and rosemary sprigs for 2 minutes. Add the rice and another splash of oil and simmer until rice becomes translucent. Add wine and let simmer, stirring constantly. Remove the rosemary sprigs. Next, add a ladleful of vegetable stock to the rice and stir until the liquid is fully absorbed. When the rice appears almost dry, add another ladleful of stock and repeat the process. Continue adding stock and stirring the rice until all of the liquid is absorbed. As it cooks, the rice will take on a creamy consistency, but it still needs to be a bit firm. Remove from heat and season with salt, pepper, Parmesan cheese and butter.

Preparation time: 2.5 hours

SALMON FILET

1.3 lb. (600 g) skinned salmon filet
Cranberry horseradish (mix one small jar of horseradish
with 3 tbsp. jellied cranberry sauce)
1 pink grapefruit
Juice of half a lemon
1 sprig rosemary
Pink salt
2 tsp. freshly cracked pink peppercorns
Olive oil

Remove pin bones from the salmon filet and cut off any brown layers. Drizzle with lemon juice and season with salt and cracked pink pepper. Next, cut into four even pieces. Grease an ovenproof casserole dish with olive oil and then add a decent splash of oil. Line up the salmon filets (place them close to each other so the fish stays juicy). Spread a ¼ inch (0.5 cm) thick layer of the cranberry horseradish over the filets. Peel the grapefruit and cut into slices. Place the grapefruit slices around the fish and use half of a slice of grapefruit to top each filet. Do not use all of the slices because you'll need some for garnish. Sprinkle rosemary over the filets and cover loosely with parchment paper.
Preheat oven to 350 °F/180 °C/gas 4. Bake salmon for 15–20 minutes. Remove fish from the casserole dish and garnish with the remaining grapefruit slices. Serve with the risotto and the relish.

Preparation time:
30 minutes + 20 minutes baking time

PAN-FRIED PRAWNS

12 prawns
3 garlic cloves
2 tbsp. rosé wine
Lemon juice
Olive oil

Peel and slice garlic. In a frying pan, heat olive oil and fry prawns (with skin). After 2 minutes, turn over the prawns and add garlic slices. When prawns turn pink, add a splash of the rosé wine and turn off the heat. Drizzle with lemon juice and serve immediately.

Preparation time: 10 minutes

Total preparation time:
3 hours and 40 minutes + 20 minutes baking time

Dessert

STRAWBERRY
AND CREAM SWISS ROLL

DOUGH

2.8 oz. (80 g) cake (soft) flour
2 ½ tbsp. (20 g) cornstarch (cornflour)
½ cup (100 g) white sugar
6 eggs
3 tbsp. red beet (beetroot) juice

FILLING

1 lb. (500 g) strawberries
17 fl. oz. (500 ml) whipping cream
½ cup (100 g) white sugar

Line a baking tray with parchment paper. Preheat oven to 425 °F/220 °C/gas 7. Separate eggs. Beat egg yolks with red beet juice and ¼ cup (50 g) of sugar until foamy. Beat the egg whites with the remaining ¼ cup (50 g) of sugar until stiff. Heap the stiff egg whites onto the egg yolk mixture and then sift the flour and the cornstarch over the egg mixture. Carefully fold in together with a wooden spoon. Spread dough over the baking tray and bake on the middle rack for about 8 to 12 minutes. In the meantime, place a clean kitchen towel on a flat surface and dust with sugar. When the dough is cooked, immediately loosen from the tray and turn cake onto prepared towel. Cover with a damp kitchen towel and let cool before carefully removing the parchment paper. Wash, dry and hull the strawberries, then cut into small pieces and add about ⅓ to a blender and purée. Beat whipping cream with a ½ cup of sugar until stiff and then mix this with the strawberry pieces and the strawberry purée. Spread the mixture over the dough. Finally, roll up cake and towel together, starting with the narrow end. Gently remove towel. To serve, cut into thick slices and place on a dessert plate.

Preparation time: 1 hour

Digestif

ROSÉ WINE

At least 1 bottle of rosé wine, e.g. Syrah

Serve chilled in white wine glasses.

Apéritif

STRAWBERRY PUNCH

1.5 lb. (750 g) fresh strawberries
1 bottle dry rosé wine
1 bottle rosé sparkling wine
5 tbsp. triple sec

Thoroughly wash strawberries, dab dry, remove the stems and caps. Put aside 8 of the strawberries. Cut the remaining strawberries into slices and place in a punch bowl. Add the triple sec and let stand for 60 minutes. Next, add the rosé wine and the sparkling wine. Garnish each glass with a strawberry. To do this, cut a tiny slit at the bottom of the berry, then place it on the rim of the glass. Repeat with the remaining berries. Pour punch into glasses and serve.

Preparation time: 15 minutes + 1 hour marinating time

Drink

RHUBARB SPRITZER

33.8 fl. oz. (1 l) rhubarb juice
33.8 fl. oz. (1 l) sparkling mineral water

Combine both beverages in a large pitcher. Serve cold.

Preparation time: 5 minutes

06

INGREDIENTS

1 small fresh red beet (beetroot)
1 lb. (500 g) mixed vegetables, e.g. red carrots,
celeriac, parsley root
1 small onion
2 red onions
6 garlic cloves

½ red chili pepper
1.6 oz. (45 g) fresh ginger
3 sprigs rosemary

3 lb. (750 g) fresh strawberries
5.5 lb. (2.5 kg) watermelon
¼ cantaloupe
10.5 oz. (300 g) rhubarb
3 fresh figs
1 pink grapefruit
1 ½ limes
1 lemon

2 cloves
2 bay leaves
Pink salt
Freshly ground pink pepper and some whole pink peppercorns
2 tsp. freshly cracked pink peppercorns
Freshly ground white pepper

1.3 lb. (600 g) skinned salmon filet
12 prawns
8 slices serrano ham
6 eggs

17 fl. oz. (500 ml) whipping cream
2.7 fl. oz. (80 ml) heavy (double) cream
Butter
1 cup (100 g) ground Parmesan cheese

1 tsp. white balsamic vinegar
½ tsp. Balsamico di Modena
Olive oil
Sunflower oil
3 tbsp. red beet (beetroot) juice
1 ½ tsp. acacia honey
1 small jar of horseradish
3 tbsp. jellied cranberry sauce

10.5 oz. (300 g) Arborio rice
2.8 oz. (80 g) cake (soft) flour
2 ½ tbsp. (20 g) cornstarch (cornflour)
½ cup (100 g) white sugar
½ cup (100 g) cane (brown) sugar
¼ cup (20 g) sliced almonds

3 bottles dry red wine
1 bottle rosé sparkling wine
5 tbsp. triple sec
1–2 tbsp. red grape juice
33.8 fl. oz. (1 l) rhubarb juice
33.8 fl. oz. (1 l) sparkling mineral water

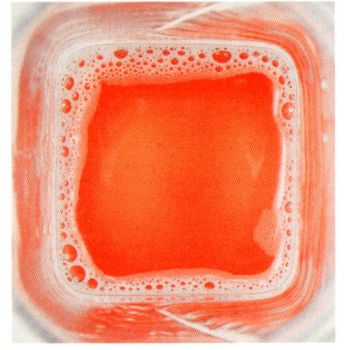

01

02

04

03

01 Drink 02 Appetizer 03 Apéritif 04 Hors d'oeuvre

05

06

07

05 Main course   06 Digestif   07 Dessert

MENU

07

Apéritif

BASIL LIME SMASH

Appetizer

**ARUGULA (ROCKET) SALAD
WITH PISTACHIO-CILANTRO
(CORIANDER) MEATBALLS**

Hors d'oeuvre

**SWISS CHARD ROLLS
WITH HERBED CREAM SAUCE**

Drink

PEPPERMINT LEMONADE

Main course

SPINACH LASAGNE

Dessert

GREEN BROWNIES

Digestif

WHEATGRASS JUICE

Appetizer

ARUGULA (ROCKET) SALAD WITH PISTACHIO-CILANTRO (CORIANDER) MEATBALLS

5.2 oz. (150 g) arugula (rocket) leaves

MEATBALLS
8 oz. (250 g) ground (minced) meat
(a mixture of beef and pork)
⅛ cup (20 g) shelled pistachios
½ bunch cilantro (coriander)
0.7 oz. (20 g) fresh ginger
1 garlic clove
6 green peppercorns
1 egg
Salt
Olive oil

DRESSING
6 tbsp. pumpkin seed oil
1 tsp. acacia honey
Juice of 1 lemon
Salt
Freshly ground black pepper

Thoroughly wash the arugula (rocket) leaves and arrange on four plates. Finely chop pistachios and green peppercorns. Wash the cilantro and shake dry. Remove the leaves and finely dice them (discard the stems). Peel and finely grate the garlic and ginger. Next, with your hands, mix the ground (minced) meat, pistachios, cilantro, garlic, ginger and peppercorns with the egg and knead into a dough. Season with salt. Roll into balls 1.2 inches in diameter. Heat oil in a pan and fry meatballs over medium heat for about 10 minutes, turning them occasionally. Remove meatballs from pan, cut them into ¾ inch pieces and place them on top of the arugula.

In a small mixing bowl, combine all dressing ingredients and mix well with a whisk. Drizzle the dressing over the arugula and the meatballs.

Preparation time: 40 minutes

Hors d'oeuvre

SWISS CHARD ROLLS
WITH HERBED CREAM SAUCE

---

12 large Swiss chard leaves

FILLING
10.5 oz. (300 g) white spelt flour
2 eggs
8.5 fl. oz. (250 ml) milk
1 bunch parsley (flat-leaf)
1 bunch chives
2 sprigs lovage
2 sprigs fresh mint
Freshly ground nutmeg
1 tbs. salt
Freshly ground green pepper

CREAM SAUCE
1 cup (250 ml) heavy (double) cream
3.4 fl. oz. (100 ml) vegetable stock
2 bunches fresh mixed herbs, e.g. parsley, chives,
mint, lovage, basil, hyssop, thyme, marjoram
Freshly ground nutmeg
Salt
Freshly ground green pepper

Approx. 24 toothpicks

For the filling, separate the eggs. Remove parsley, lovage and mint leaves from the stems. Dice and mix with chopped chives. Set aside.

In a large bowl, combine flour, green pepper and nutmeg. Use a smaller bowl to mix egg yolk and milk, and then pour the egg mixture over the seasoned flour. Work the dough into a smooth mass using an electric hand mixer (with a dough hook) until it is nice and shiny and small bubbles are visible. Cover the dough with a clean kitchen towel and let stand at room temperature for 30 minutes. In the meantime, wash the Swiss chard leaves, remove stems and center ribs. Pound thicker leaf veins until flat. Blanch the leaves for about 1 minute in boiling water, one at a time. Place leaves on a paper towel and dab dry.

Mix the finely diced herbs with the dough. Beat egg whites and salt until stiff and then carefully fold into the dough. Next, place one tablespoon of dough onto each leaf. Fold the sides of the leaf up over the filling, then roll up the leaf, enclosing the filling completely (like a burrito). Carefully secure rolls with toothpicks. Repeat with each leaf.

For the herbed cream sauce, combine ¾ cup (200 ml) of heavy (double) cream and 1.7 fl. oz. (50 ml) of vegetable stock in a large frying pan and bring to a boil. Reduce heat, place the Swiss chard rolls in the sauce and let each portion simmer for about 8–10 minutes. Remove rolls from the pan and carefully pull out the toothpicks. Add the mixed herbs plus the remaining cream and broth to the sauce and simmer over low heat for 5 minutes.

Finally, place Swiss chard rolls on plates and pour the herbed cream sauce over the rolls.

Preparation time:
1 hour + 30 minutes standing time

Main course

SPINACH LASAGNE

12 green lasagne sheets

GREEN TOMATO SAUCE
2.2 lb. (1 kg) green tomatoes
2 onions
Salt
Freshly ground black pepper
One pinch sugar
Olive oil

PESTO
2 bunches basil
¼ cup (25 g) shelled pistachios
¼ cup (25 g) pumpkin seeds
1.7 oz. (50 g) Parmesan cheese
2 garlic cloves
5 fl. oz. (150 ml) olive oil
Salt

FILLING
1.5 lb. (750 g) spinach leaves or frozen spinach
½ cup (50 g) pumpkin seeds
3.5 oz. (100 g) ricotta cheese
4.4 oz. (125 g) crème fraîche
4 garlic cloves
2 tbsp. butter
Freshly ground nutmeg
Salt
Freshly ground black pepper
Olive oil

1 tbsp. butter (to grease pan)
2.6 oz. (75 g) pesto cheese
2 tbsp. bread crumbs
2 tbsp. butter flakes

For the tomato sauce, peel and dice the onions. Wash the tomatoes and cut them into small pieces. Heat olive oil in a saucepan and sauté onions until they are translucent. Add the tomatoes and a pinch of salt and bring to a boil. Cover with a lid, lower the heat and simmer for 30 minutes. Use a hand blender and purée the tomato sauce. Season with salt, pepper and sugar.

For the pesto, cut Parmesan into small pieces and remove the basil leaves from the stems. In a blender, combine pistachios, pumpkin seeds, salt, Parmesan and garlic cloves with oil and blend until smooth. Finally, add the basil leaves and blend for just a few more seconds.

For the spinach filling, peel and grate the garlic. Thoroughly wash the spinach. Melt butter in a wide saucepan and briefly sauté the garlic, then add the spinach and sauté until spinach starts to wilt (about 10 minutes). Drain excess liquid.
Next, chop the pumpkin seeds. Mix seeds with ricotta, crème fraîche and spinach. Season with salt and pepper (use a decent amount!) and mix until smooth.

Grease an ovenproof dish and cover the bottom with one
layer of lasagne sheets. Pour a portion of the tomato
sauce over the sheets, then spread a layer of pesto on top.
Follow with the spinach filling and another layer of
lasagne noodles. Continue until all of the lasagne
sheets have been used, and finish with a final layer of
tomato sauce.

Grate the pesto cheese and mix with the bread crumbs.
Spread butter flakes over the lasagne and cover with
the cheese. Preheat oven to 400 °F/200 °C/gas 6 and
bake for 45 minutes.

Preparation time:
1.5 hours + 45 minutes baking time

Dessert

GREEN BROWNIES

1.4 oz. (40 g) matcha green tea powder (Japanese tea powder)
8 oz. (250 g) white chocolate
3.5 oz. (100 g) butter
½ cup (100 g) cane (brown) sugar
1 cup (100 g) all-purpose flour
½ tsp. baking powder
2 eggs
¼ cup (50 ml) heavy (double) cream
1 pinch salt

Coarsely grate 200 g (7 oz.) of the chocolate and chop the remaining into small pieces. Over low heat, melt butter and grated chocolate. Slowly pour in the cream and mix, then let cool. In a bowl, beat eggs, matcha and sugar until foamy. Whisk the chocolate mixture into egg mixture and allow to cool for 20 minutes before adding the remaining 50 g (1 oz.) of chocolate. Combine flour and baking powder, sieve it over the chocolate dough and carefully fold it in.
Line a 12–14 inch loaf pan with parchment paper and pour in the dough. Bake for 30 minutes at 320 °F/160 °C/gas 3. The cake should still be a bit juicy! Let cool, cut into pieces and serve.

Preparation time: 30 minutes + 20 minutes standing time + 30 minutes baking time

Apéritif

BASIL LIME SMASH

6.6 oz. (20 cl) gin
2 bunches basil
2.6 oz. (8 cl) lime juice, freshly squeezed (approx. 3 limes)
2.6 oz. (8 cl) agave syrup
Crushed ice

For each cocktail, in a blender, mix about 20 fresh basil leaves with 0.6 oz. (2 cl) of lime juice and then pour into a cocktail shaker. Add 1.6 oz. (5 cl) of gin and 0.6 oz. (2 cl) of agave syrup plus a handful of crushed ice and shake for 10 seconds. Strain into a cocktail glass.

Preparation time: 15 minutes

Digestif

WHEATGRASS JUICE

---

8 oz. (250 g) fresh organic wheatgrass
or bottled, organic wheatgrass juice

Cut off the wheatgrass with a pair of scissors and mix it in a power-juicer. Pour juice into small shot glasses. Drink immediately.

Preparation time: 10 minutes

Drink

PEPPERMINT LEMONADE

---

4 bunches fresh mint
1.5 lb. (700 g) fresh pineapple
2 limes
3 oranges
4 tbsp. white sugar
33.8 fl. oz. (1 l) sparkling mineral water

Thoroughly wash the mint, then remove the leaves from the stalks and roughly chop them. Cut the pineapple into quarters, remove the skin and the core, and then cut into slices. In a blender, squeeze limes and oranges and mix the juice with the chopped mint leaves, pineapple slices and sugar. Refrigerate for 2 hours. Pour juice into a pitcher and add the sparkling water. Serve immediately.

Preparation time:
30 minutes + 2 hours cooling time

INGREDIENTS

1.5 lb. (750 g) spinach leaves or frozen spinach
12 large Swiss chard leaves
2.2 lb. (1 kg) green tomatoes
5.2 oz. (150 g) arugula (rocket) leaves
2 onions
7 garlic cloves
0.7 oz. (20 g) fresh ginger
4 bunches fresh mint
4 bunches basil
½ bunch cilantro (coriander)
1 bunch parsley (flat-leaf)
1 bunch chives
2 sprigs lovage
2 bunches fresh mixed herbs, e.g. parsley, chives, mint,
lovage, basil, hyssop, thyme, marjoram
8 oz. (250 g) fresh organic wheatgrass or bottled,
organic wheatgrass juice

1.5 lb. (700 g) fresh pineapple
5 limes
3 oranges
1 lemon

6 green peppercorns
Freshly ground nutmeg
Salt
Freshly ground black pepper

8 oz. (250 g) ground (minced) meat (a mixture
of beef and pork)
5 eggs

8.5 fl. oz. (250 ml) milk
1 ¼ cup (250 ml) heavy (double) cream
3.5 oz. (100 g) ricotta cheese
4.4 oz. (125 g) crème fraîche
7 oz. (200 g) butter
2.6 oz. (75 g) pesto cheese
1.7 oz. (50 g) Parmesan cheese

3.4 fl. oz. (100 ml) vegetable stock
6.7 fl. oz. (200 ml) olive oil
6 tbsp. pumpkin seed oil
1 tsp. acacia honey
2.6 oz. (8 cl) agave syrup

12 green lasagne sheets
10.5 oz. (300 g) white spelt flour
1 cup (100 g) all-purpose flour
2 tbsp. bread crumbs
½ tsp. baking powder
½ cup (100 g) cane (brown) sugar
4 tbsp. white sugar
⅜ cup (45 g) shelled pistachios
¾ cup (75 g) pumpkin seeds
1.4 oz. (40 g) matcha green tea powder (Japanese
tea powder)
8 oz. (250 g) white chocolate

6.6 oz. (20 cl) gin
33.8 fl. oz. (1 l) sparkling mineral water

Crushed ice
Approx. 24 toothpicks

01

03

02

04

06

05

07

04 Dessert 05 Digestif 06 Main course 07 Appetizer

MENU
08

Apéritif

SANGRIA

Appetizer

GAZPACHO

Hors d'oeuvre

BRUSCHETTA

Drink

ICED FRUIT TEA

Main course

STUFFED BELL PEPPERS

Dessert

RED CURRANT TARTELETTES

Digestif

RED CURRANT LIQUEUR

Appetizer

GAZPACHO

---

1 lb. (500 g) fresh tomatoes (or canned tomatoes)
3 red bell peppers
2 tbsp. sherry vinegar
1 garlic clove
4 tbsp. olive oil
1 pinch sugar
Red salt
Freshly ground red pepper
Ice cubes

Cut a cross into the skin on one side of the tomatoes, pour boiling water over them and peel off the skins. Cut tomatoes into eighths. Preheat oven to 428 °F/220 °C/ gas 7. Line a baking tray with parchment paper. Wash bell peppers, remove the seeds and cut in quarters. Place bell peppers skin side up on the sheet and roast for 25 to 30 minutes or until the skin turns light brown and blisters. Next, remove peppers from the oven and cover them with a damp paper towel. Once the bell peppers are cool, peel off the skins. Peel garlic. In a blender, combine tomatoes, bell peppers, sherry vinegar, garlic, oil and sugar and blend to a smooth, creamy liquid. Add 2 to 3 ice cubes. Pour gazpacho into a bowl, cover and place in the fridge for at least 4 hours. Just before serving, season to taste with spices and vinegar.

Preparation time:
45 minutes + 4 hours marinating time

Hors d'oeuvre

BRUSCHETTA

CIABATTA
3 ½ cups (450 g) all purpose flour
½ cube (20 g) fresh yeast
13.2 fl. oz. (300 ml) lukewarm water
2 tsp. sugar
2 tsp. salt
2 tbsp. olive oil
1 tube tomato paste (7 oz./200 g)

TOPPING
8 large, ripe tomatoes
1.7 fl. oz. (50 ml) white balsamic vinegar
1.7 fl. oz. (50 ml) red wine
1.7 fl. oz. (50 ml) red grape juice
2 tbsp. honey
1 garlic clove
Red salt
Freshly ground red pepper
Olive oil

For the ciabatta, sift flour into a bowl. Make a well in the center of the flour. Dissolve sugar and crumbled yeast in 13.2 fl. oz. (300 ml) of lukewarm water and pour into the well. Dust the mixture with the flour and knead into a smooth dough. Cover with a towel and set in a warm place for at least 30 minutes or until the dough has risen considerably. Add salt, oil and tomato paste and knead back into a smooth dough.

Line a baking tray with parchment paper. Shape dough into a loaf and let rise for 30 more minutes, or until dough has doubled in size. Preheat oven to 446 °F/230 °C/gas 8 and bake for 30 minutes until golden brown.

Meanwhile, cut a cross into the tomato skins on one side, pour boiling water over them and peel off the skins. Next, cut tomatoes in half, remove the seeds, cut into small pieces and let drain in a sieve. Season with 1 tbsp. of olive oil and salt and pepper.

For the balsamic vinegar cream, combine vinegar with red wine and bring to a boil, stirring constantly. As soon as the mixture begins to thicken, add grape juice and honey and return to a boil. Simmer until cream thickens. Remove from heat and let cool.

Cut ciabatta into ¾ inch wide slices and roast in the oven at 356 °F/180 °C/gas 4 for about 5 minutes. Remove slices from the oven and rub a whole garlic clove over one side of the bread. Drizzle with olive oil and spread a little bit of the balsamic vinegar cream over each slice. Top generously with tomatoes.

Preparation time: 1 hour + 1 hour rising time
+ 35 minutes baking time

Main course

STUFFED BELL PEPPERS

VEGETABLE STOCK
1.5 lb. (750 g) mixed red and white vegetables,
e.g. tomatoes, red bell peppers, carrots, celeriac, parsnips
2 red onions
1 garlic clove
2 bay leaves
50.7 fl. oz. (1.5 l) water
Salt
Freshly ground red pepper
Sunflower oil

BELL PEPPERS
4 large red bell peppers
12.3 oz. (350 g) mixed ground (minced) meat (equal parts
beef and pork)
³/₄ cup (150 g) rice (long grain, uncooked)
3.4 fl. oz. (100 ml) white wine
2 tbsp. tomato paste
2 small onions
2 garlic cloves
½ tsp. ground cumin
½ tsp. ground chili
Red salt
Freshly ground red pepper
Olive oil

SAUCE
²/₃ cup (150 ml) tomato paste
2 tbsp. bell pepper paste
2 onions
3 garlic cloves
1 tsp. bell pepper powder
Red salt
Freshly ground red pepper
1 pinch sugar
Olive oil

For the vegetable stock, wash and dice vegetables. Chop all the other ingredients. Heat oil in a large saucepan and briefly fry the vegetables. Add 50.7 fl. oz. (1.5 l) of water and let simmer for about 40 minutes over low heat or until the liquid has reduced by half. Remove from heat and let cool for 20 minutes. Pass stock through a fine sieve and season with salt. Use immediately.

Meanwhile, wash the bell peppers. Carefully cut out the stems, leaving a small opening. Next, remove the seeds and set the peppers aside. Peel and dice onions and garlic and fry in olive oil until translucent. Add the rice and let simmer for 3 minutes. Add white wine and reduce liquid. Add 8.4 fl. oz. (250 ml) of the vegetable stock and let simmer for 10 more minutes. Remove from the stove and mix with ground (minced) meat, cumin, ground chili, salt and pepper. Stir in the tomato paste. Fill the bell peppers with the meat-rice mix. Make sure to leave room (¼ of the peppers) for the rice to expand.

For the sauce, peel and dice onions and garlic and let simmer until translucent in a tall, wide saucepan. Stir in 1 tbsp. ground bell pepper. Add 17 fl. oz. (500 ml) of the vegetable stock, then add the tomato and bell pepper paste and season with salt, pepper and sugar. Stand the stuffed bell peppers in the sauce, cover with a lid and let simmer for 40 minutes. Reduce the heat and let peppers cool for 10 minutes. To serve, spread some sauce on a plate and place one bell pepper on each plate.

Preparation time: 2.5 hours

Dessert

RED CURRANT TARTELETTES

7 oz. (200 g) red currants (without stems)
1 cup (125 g) cake flour
2.1 oz. (60 g) butter
1 small egg
1 pinch baking powder
2 tbsp. (30 g) sugar
⅓ cup (40 g) gelling (jam) sugar
1 pinch salt
1 squeeze lemon
Butter

4 tart moulds (tart cases) (Ø 3 inches/8 cm)

Combine flour, baking powder, sugar and salt. Add the egg and soft butter pieces and knead into a dough. Shape into a ball and wrap in plastic, then place in the fridge for 30 minutes. Meanwhile, purée 5.2 oz. (150 g) of red currants and press through a sieve. In a saucepan, mix berry purée (approx. 3.5 oz./100 g) with ⅓ cup (40 g) of gelling sugar and a squeeze of lemon juice and bring to a boil. Cook for 3 minutes and, if necessary, skim off any foam. Next, fold in the remaining berries. Preheat oven to 400 °F/200 °C/gas 6. On a sheet of parchment paper, roll out a thin layer of dough and cut out 4 discs (approx. Ø 4 inches/10 cm). Grease the tart moulds with butter and dust with flour. Press discs into each tart mould using your thumb, poke several holes in the dough with a fork and cut off any excess dough. Place moulds on a baking tray on the middle oven rack and bake for 15 minutes. Remove from oven and allow to cool. Carefully remove tartelettes from moulds. Spread red currant filing onto the tartelettes.

Preparation time: 1 hour + 15 minutes baking time
+ 30 minutes cooling time

Apéritif

SANGRIA

25.3 fl. oz. (0.75 l) rosé wine
8.4 fl. oz. (0.25 l) dry red wine
1 fl. oz. (30 ml) red port wine
1.7 fl. oz. (50 ml) triple sec
2 organic blood oranges
2 organic pink grapefruits
3 nectarines
¼ watermelon
2 tsp. cane (brown) sugar
10 ice cubes

Thoroughly wash oranges, grapefruits and nectarines and dab dry. Do not peel. Cut into small pieces and remove nectarine pits. Dice melon and combine all fruit in a large punch bowl. Sweeten with sugar. Add port wine and triple sec and mix well with a spoon. Add wine and place sangria in the fridge for at least two hours. Just before serving, add the ice cubes. Serve with cocktail spears for the fruit.

Preparation time: 15 minutes + 2 hours infusing time

Drink

ICED FRUIT TEA

---

5 tbsp. dried red fruits, e.g. rose hips, strawberries, cherries, hibiscus etc.
1 vanilla bean
2 tbsp. honey
67.6 fl. oz. (2 l) water
Ice cubes

Bring water to a boil. Add dried fruits and vanilla bean and bring to a boil again and then remove from heat. Let steep for 15 minutes. Sweeten with honey and let cool. Serve with ice cubes.

Preparation time: 20 minutes

Digestif

RED CURRANT LIQUEUR

Ingredients will make enough to fill a large jar (67.6 fl. oz./2 l)

17.6 oz. (500 g) red currants (without stems)
25.3 fl. oz. (0.75 l) fruit brandy (e.g. cherry)
1 ½ cups (300 g) cane (brown) sugar
3 cloves
1 cinnamon stick

Wash and drain red currants. In a wide, flat bowl, mash currants with a potato masher. Combine with sugar in a large sealable glass jar, cover and infuse over night. Next, add the cinnamon stick and the cloves and the fruit brandy. Tightly close the lid, shake well and keep in a warm place for at least 2 months, shaking every once in a while. After 2 months, strain liqueur through a coffee or tea filter into glass bottles, carefully squeezing the berries to keep the seeds from falling into the liqueur.

Preparation time: 20 minutes + 2 months infusing time

O8

INGREDIENTS

---

7 large red bell peppers

8 large, ripe tomatoes

1 lb. (500 g) fresh tomatoes (or canned tomatoes)

1.5 lb. (750 g) mixed red and white vegetables,

e.g. tomatoes, red bell peppers, carrots, celeriac, parsnips

2 onions

2 small onions

2 red onions

8 garlic cloves

1.5 lb. (700 g) red currants (without stems)

2 organic blood oranges

2 organic pink grapefruits

3 nectarines

1/4 watermelon

1 lemon

2 bay leaves

1/2 tsp. ground cumin

1/2 tsp. ground chili

1 tsp. bell pepper powder

3 cloves

1 cinnamon stick

1 vanilla bean

Salt

Red salt

Freshly ground red pepper

12.3 oz. (350 g) mixed ground (minced) meat (equal parts beef and pork)

1 small egg

2.1 oz. (60 g) butter

120 ml olive oil

Sunflower oil

1.7 fl. oz. (50 ml) white balsamic vinegar

2 tbsp. sherry vinegar

4 tbsp. honey

2 tubes tomato paste (14 oz./400 g)

2 tbsp. bell pepper paste

3/4 cup (150 g) rice (long grain, uncooked)

3 1/2 cups (450 g) all purpose flour

1 cup (125 g) cake flour

1 pinch baking powder

1 1/2 cup (300 g) cane (brown) sugar

2 tbsp. (30 g) sugar

1/3 cup (40 g) gelling (jam) sugar

1/2 cube (20 g) fresh yeast

5 tbsp. dried red fruits, e.g. rose hips, strawberries, cherries, hibiscus etc.

3.4 fl. oz. (100 ml) white wine

1.7 fl. oz. (50 ml) red wine

1.7 fl. oz. (50 ml) red grape juice

25.3 fl. oz. (0.75 l) fruit brandy (e.g. cherry)

25.3 fl. oz. (0.75 l) rosé wine

8.4 fl. oz. (0.25 l) dry red wine

1 fl. oz. (30 ml) red port wine

1.7 fl. oz. (50 ml) triple sec

Ice cubes

4 tart moulds (tart cases) (Ø 3 inches/8 cm)

01

02

03

04

01 Hors d'oeuvre 02 Appetizer 03 Apéritif 04 Drink

05

06

07

MENU

09

Apéritif

**LAVENDER LEMONADE
WITH VIOLET FLOWER ICE CUBES**

Appetizer

RED CABBAGE SOUP

Hors d'oeuvre

**VIOLET POTATO CHIPS
WITH BLACKBERRIES**

Drink

VIOLET MOON COCKTAIL

Main course

BLUE TORTILLAS

Dessert

BLUEBERRY TARTELETTES

Digestif

VIOLET SMOOTHIE

Appetizer

RED CABBAGE SOUP

VEGETABLE STOCK

1 lb. (500 g) mixed purple and white vegetables,
e.g. purple carrots, celeriac, parsnip, white leaves of leek
1 red onion
1 garlic clove
1 clove
2 bay leaves
40.6 fl. oz. (1.2 l) water
Salt
Freshly ground black pepper
Olive oil

SOUP

1 medium-sized red cabbage
2 sweet, juicy apples
2 sweet, juicy pears
2 onions
3.4 fl. oz. (100 ml) heavy (double) cream
1 ½ tbsp. (20 g) butter
4 bay leaves
Freshly ground nutmeg
Salt
Freshly ground black pepper

For the vegetable stock, wash and dice the vegetables. Coarsely chop the remaining ingredients. Heat olive oil in a large saucepan and add the vegetables. Briefly fry, and then add 40.6 fl. oz. (1.2 l) of water and simmer for 50 minutes over low heat, or until the liquid has reduced by one half. Remove from stove and let cool for 20 minutes. Next, pass stock through a fine sieve and season with salt. Use immediately.

In a juicer, add cabbage pieces and juice. Peel the apples and the pears and cut into small cubes. Finely chop the onions. Heat butter and sauté onions until translucent, and then add the vegetable stock and the red cabbage juice. Season with bay leaves, nutmeg and salt and cook for 15 minutes. Finally, add the cream and blend. Season with salt and pepper.

Preparation time: 1.5 hours

Hors d'oeuvre

VIOLET POTATO CHIPS WITH BLACKBERRIES

1.3 lb. (600 g) purple potatoes, e.g. Vitelotte
1 ½ cups (250 g) blackberries
8.4 fl. oz. (250 ml) peanut oil
Salt

Peel potatoes and cut into paper-thin slices. For the best results, use a regular mandoline or meat slicer. Dust slices with some flour. Heat peanut oil in a frying pan and fry potato chips until they start to turn golden brown. Drain single chips on paper towels and sprinkle with salt. Serve with fresh blackberries.

Preparation time: 45 minutes

Main course

BLUE TORTILLAS

TORTILLAS

2 cups (300 g) blue cornmeal

1 ¼ cup (150 g) cake (plain) flour

1 small egg

½ tsp. salt

Corn oil

Milk, if necessary

FRIJOLES

2 small cans (16 oz./450 g) kidney beans

2 onions

2 garlic cloves

1 chili pepper

Salt

Freshly ground black pepper

Butter

VEGETABLE FILLING

1 purple bell pepper

6 purple potatoes, e.g. Vitelotte

4 purple carrots

1 red onion

1 garlic clove

¼ tsp. ground coriander

Salt

Freshly ground black pepper

3 tbsp. olive oil

1 bunch purple basil

SALSA

¾ cup (200 ml) chicken stock

2 red onions

2 garlic cloves

1 purple potato

3 tbsp. ground chili

1 tsp. ground cumin

¼ tsp. ground oregano

¼ tsp. ground cinnamon

Salt

Freshly ground pepper

3 tbsp. olive oil

Red radish sprouts

For the tortillas, combine cornmeal and flour, salt and egg and mix into a batter that is thin enough to pour easily. If the batter is too thick, add some milk. Next, add a tablespoon of corn oil and let batter stand for 20 minutes. Heat some oil in a frying pan, pour in the batter and bake tortillas on both sides over low heat. Since they should remain blue, do not cook for too long (or they will turn brown).

For the frijoles, purée canned beans (including the liquid) in a blender. Finely chop the onion, garlic and chili and fry in some butter until translucent. Add the bean purée and let simmer for 10 minutes over low heat, stirring constantly. Season to taste with salt and pepper.

For the vegetable filling, finely chop bell pepper, potatoes and carrots. Remove the basil leaves from the stems and set aside. Peel and dice onion and garlic and fry in some olive oil until translucent. Add the vegetables and fry for a few minutes until tender, but still a bit firm. Season with ground coriander, salt and pepper. Finally, add the basil leaves.

For the salsa, finely grate the raw potato. Peel and dice the onions and garlic and fry in some olive oil. Add the spices and let simmer for a few minutes, stirring constantly. Add the grated potato and the ground chili and mix well, and then add the chicken stock and stir. Let sauce reduce to desired consistency.

Spread frijoles onto the baked tortillas, add the vegetable filling and drizzle with salsa. Next, fold the sides of each tortilla toward the center and garnish each one with radish sprouts.

Preparation time:
2.5 hours + 20 minutes standing time

Dessert

BLUEBERRY TARTELETTES

TOPPING
³⁄₈ cup (40 g) blueberries

FILLING
1 ½ cups (150 g) blueberries
3.5 oz. (100 g) mascarpone
3.5 oz. (100 g) cream cheese
2 tbsp. honey
1 tbsp. lemon juice
2 gelatin sheets

CRUST
¼ cup (25 g) blueberries
⅓ cup (50 g) roasted and ground almonds
¼ cup (25 g) ground Brazil nuts
¼ cup (25 g) dates
½ tbsp. almond oil
1 tsp. agave syrup
1 pinch salt

4 paper cups Ø 2.7 inch/7 cm

For the crust, blend almonds, nuts, dates and the blueberries in a blender. Add oil, agave syrup and salt and mix well. Cut off the bottoms of the paper cups, leaving a 1.5 inch rim. Place your paper 'ramekins' on a flat plate lined with parchment paper and press the nut mixture into the ramekins. This will be your bottom crust.

For the filling, soak the gelatin sheets in a little cold water until soft. Meanwhile, purée the blueberries and then, using a whisk, mix with mascarpone, cream cheese, honey and lemon juice. Squeeze out any excess water from the softened gelatin sheets and then carefully place them in a little hot water, stirring constantly, until gelatin has fully dissolved. Next, slowly pour liquid gelatin into the blueberry mascarpone mixture, stir well and spread onto the bottom crust. Place in the fridge for at least 4 hours or until stiff. After two hours, remove the ramekins from the fridge and place blueberries on top, and then return to the fridge. To serve, cut the ramekins open and place the tartelettes on dessert plates.

Preparation time: 1 hour + 4 hours cooling time

VIOLET MOON COCKTAIL

---

2 cups (250 g) fresh blueberries
5.4 fl. oz. (16 cl) Crème de Violette (clear)
2.7 fl. oz. (8 cl) gin
0.7 oz. (20 g) sugar
7.4 fl. oz. (220 ml) water

For the syrup, heat 0.7 oz. (20 ml) of sugar with 0.7 fl. oz. (20 ml) of water in a small saucepan and bring to a boil. Stir until sugar has dissolved and then remove from stove and let cool.

For the blueberry water, thoroughly wash blueberries and add to a small saucepan. Pour in a bit of water and bring to a boil. Simmer until blueberries fall apart and then pass through a fine sieve. Pour the blueberry water into a bowl and set aside. Next, rinse the sieve with the blueberry skins with 6.7 fl. oz. (200 ml) of water to create a violet-colored liquid.

For each cocktail, add 0.6 fl. oz. (2 cl) of gin, 1.2 fl. oz. (4 cl) of Crème de Violette, ⅓ oz. (1 cl) of syrup and crushed ice to a cocktail shaker and shake for 10 seconds. Strain into a cocktail glass and fill with 0.9 fl. oz. (3 cl) of blueberry water.

Preparation time: 30 minutes

Apéritif

LAVENDER LEMONADE WITH VIOLET FLOWER ICE CUBES

---

6 tbsp. dried lavender flowers
6–8 single violet flowers
1 cup (200 g) sugar
1 organic lemon
8.4 fl. oz. (250 ml) water
2 bottles mineral water
Ice cube tray

For the ice cubes, place violet flowers and single leaves in the ice cube tray, fill with water and freeze.

For the lemonade, wash the lemon with hot water and then juice it. Keep the lemon halves and place in a saucepan with sugar and 8.4 fl. oz. (250 ml) of water. Bring to a boil. Remove from heat and add lemon juice and lavender flowers. Let cool and infuse over night.

Strain the lemonade through a fine sieve, making sure to press on the lavender flowers and lemons with a spoon to push out all the juices. To serve, pour lemonade into a pitcher, top with sparkling water to taste and add the violet flower ice cubes.

Preparation time: 15 minutes + 12 hours infusing time + 6 hours freezing time

Digestif

VIOLET SMOOTHIE

---

1 ⅓ cups (200 g) blueberries
2 ripe bananas
3.4 fl. oz. (100 ml) plain yogurt (3.8% full fat)
8.4 fl. oz. (250 ml) whole milk
2 tbsp. honey
8 ice cubes

In a blender, add all ingredients and blend until foamy. Pour into 4 glasses.

Preparation time: 5 minutes

09

INGREDIENTS

---

1 medium-sized red cabbage
2.6 lb. (1.2 kg) purple potatoes, e.g. Vitelotte
1 lb. (500 g) mixed purple and white vegetables, e.g. purple
carrots, celeriac, parsnip, white leaves of leek
4 purple carrots
1 purple bell pepper
4 onions
4 red onions
6 garlic cloves
1 chili pepper
Red radish sprouts
1 bunch purple basil

1.4 lbs. (665 g) blueberries
1 ½ cups (250 g) blackberries
2 sweet, juicy apples
2 sweet, juicy pears
2 ripe bananas
2 organic lemons

1 clove
6 bay leaves
Freshly ground nutmeg
3 tbsp. ground chili
1 tsp. ground cumin
¼ tsp. ground oregano
¼ tsp. ground cinnamon
¼ tsp. ground coriander
Salt
Freshly ground black pepper

1 small egg

3.5 oz. (100 g) mascarpone
3.5 oz. (100 g) cream cheese
3.4 fl. oz. (100 ml) plain yogurt (3.8% full fat)
3.4 fl. oz. (100 ml) heavy (double) cream
8.4 fl. oz. (250 ml) whole milk
3 tbsp. (40 g) butter

¾ cup (200 ml) chicken stock
Olive oil
8.4 fl. oz. (250 ml) peanut oil
Corn oil
½ tbsp. almond oil
4 tbsp. honey
1 tsp. agave syrup

2 small cans (16 oz./450 g) kidney beans
2 cups (300 g) blue cornmeal
1 ¼ cup (150 g) cake (plain) flour
7.7 oz. (220 g) sugar
6 tbsp. dried lavender flowers
6–8 single violet flowers
⅓ cup (50 g) roasted and ground almonds
¼ cup (25 g) ground Brazil nuts
¼ cup (25 g) dates
2 gelatin sheets

5.4 fl. oz. (16 cl) Crème de Violette (clear)
2.7 fl. oz. (8 cl) gin
2 bottles mineral water

Ice cubes
Ice cube tray
4 paper cups Ø 2.7 inch/7 cm

01

02

03

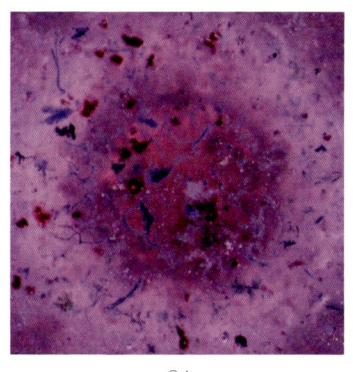

04

05

07

06

04 Drink 05 Hors d'oeuvre 06 Apéritif 07 Appetizer

MENU
10

Apéritif

KUMQUAT COCKTAIL

Appetizer

**CARROT SALAD WITH
ORANGE MUSTARD VINAIGRETTE**

Hors d'oeuvre

SWEET POTATO SOUP

Drink

ORANGE AND CARROT JUICE

Main course

**RED LENTIL PATTIES WITH
STEWED PUMPKIN AND ROASTED
BELL PEPPERS**

Dessert

**CARAMELIZED FRUIT WITH
ORANGE CHEESE**

Digestif

TANGERINE LIQUEUR

Appetizer

CARROT SALAD WITH
ORANGE MUSTARD VINAIGRETTE

1.3 lb. (600 g) carrots
3 tangerines
2 medium-sized organic oranges
2 ½ tbsp. (40 ml) canola oil
2 ½ tbsp. (40 ml) olive oil
2 tbsp. honey (e.g. orange blossom)
1 tsp. pear mustard
3 tsp. medium hot or hot mustard
(according to personal taste)
Salt
Freshly ground white pepper

Peel carrots, cut into fine sticks and arrange on plates.
Garnish with 4–6 tangerine sections. Wash and dry the
oranges and grate zest into a bowl. Add freshly squeezed
juice from the oranges, honey and canola oil. Slowly whisk
in olive oil and season with mustard, salt and pepper.

Preparation time: 30 minutes

Hors d'oeuvre

SWEET POTATO SOUP

2 large yams (sweet potatoes)
8 small carrots
1 orange
0.7 oz. (20 g) fresh ginger
2 large garlic cloves
2 tbsp. unsweetened peanut butter
$\frac{1}{2}$ tsp. chili powder
1 tsp. ground turmeric
2 tsp. orange olive oil
Salt

Peel and dice carrots. In a large saucepan, bring salted water to a boil, add the carrots and let simmer for 5 to 7 minutes. Peel yams and cut into small pieces. Next, peel and finely slice ginger and garlic. Add yams, ginger and garlic to the carrots and cook until yams are done (if necessary, add some more water when adding the vegetables). Next, remove all but 3 ginger slices, and purée the soup until smooth. Squeeze orange and add the juice and peanut butter to the soup. Season with turmeric, chili powder and oil.

Preparation time: 30 minutes

Main course

RED LENTIL PATTIES WITH STEWED PUMPKIN AND ROASTED BELL PEPPERS

STEWED PUMPKIN

2.2 lb. (1 kg) Hokkaido or Japanese squash
2 organic oranges
1 oz. (30 g) fresh ginger
1 tbsp. cane (brown) sugar
2 chili peppers
3 garlic cloves
2 cinnamon sticks
Salt
Freshly ground white pepper
6 tbsp. orange olive oil

Wash the squash, cut it in half and scoop out the seeds with a large spoon. Cut flesh into 1.2 inch (3 cm) thick pieces. Wash the oranges in hot water and dab dry. In a small bowl, grate the peel of one orange and in another bowl, squeeze out the juice of both oranges. Place the pieces of squash in a large casserole dish or on a baking sheet and season with salt, pepper, chili and sugar. Peel garlic and cut into thin slices. Place garlic, ginger, orange zest and cinnamon sticks on top of the squash. Drizzle with olive oil and orange juice. Preheat oven to 400°F/200 °C/gas 6. Cover casserole dish loosely with aluminum foil and bake for 25 minutes, then remove foil and bake for another 10 to 15 minutes.

Preparation time: 30 minutes + 40 minutes baking time

ROASTED BELL PEPPERS

4 orange bell peppers
1 tbsp. dry white wine
1 tbsp. white balsamic vinegar
3 tbsp. olive oil
2 garlic cloves
Salt
Freshly ground white pepper

Preheat oven to 428 °F/220 °C/gas 7. Line a baking sheet with parchment paper. Wash the peppers, remove the seeds and cut into quarters. Place them skin side up on the sheet and roast for 25 to 30 minutes or until the skin turns light brown and blisters. Remove peppers from oven and cover with a damp kitchen towel to cool them off. For the marinade, combine garlic, balsamic vinegar, wine, oil, salt and pepper and mix well. Using a knife, remove skin from the peppers and coat with the marinade.

Preparation time: 15 minutes + 30 minutes baking time

RED LENTIL PATTIES

7 oz. (200 g) red lentils

3.5 oz. (100 g) yams (sweet potatoes)

1 large carrot

1 medium-sized onion

6 tbsp. flour

3 tbsp. bread crumbs

1 small egg

1 garlic clove

1 tsp. harissa paste (hot chili paste)

2 tsp. tomato paste

1 tsp. garam masala (Indian spice mix)

Salt

Freshly ground white pepper

Olive oil

Bring water to a boil and cook lentils for about 10 minutes or until tender. Drain and let cool. Peel and dice onions and garlic and fry in oil until translucent. Peel and finely grate carrot and yams. In a bowl, combine lentils with egg, flour, bread crumbs, grated carrot and yams, onion, garlic, pastes and spices and mix to form a smooth dough. Season with salt and pepper. Next, heat oil in a frying pan. Take one tablespoon of dough at a time and shape it into a small ball. Carefully flatten into a disc. Add the patties to the hot oil. Over low heat, briefly fry on both sides until the patties are golden brown. Remove from pan and drain on paper towels.

Preparation time: 45 minutes

Total preparation time:

1.5 hours + 70 minutes baking time

Dessert

CARAMELIZED FRUIT WITH ORANGE CHEESE

---

16 physalis

8 apricots

8 medlars

8 kumquats

5.2 oz. (150 g) Red Leicester cheese

⅛ cup (30 g) white sugar

2 tbsp. lemon juice

1.7 fl. oz. (50 ml) water

Wash all fruit and dab dry. Depending on size, either cut in half or into quarters. In a small saucepan, heat sugar and allow to caramelize, stirring constantly. Add water, then add lemon juice and let simmer for one minute, again stirring all the time. Now add the fruit and swivel the pan to cover everything with the caramel sauce. Place on dessert plates and serve with thin slices of the cheese.

Preparation time: 20 minutes

Apéritif

KUMQUAT COCKTAIL

***

4.4 oz. (125 g) kumquats
3.4 fl. oz. (100 ml) triple sec
3.4 fl. oz. (100 ml) cachaça
2.7 fl. oz. (80 ml) fresh lime juice (approx. 4 limes)
4 tbsp. agave syrup
Ice cubes

Wash kumquats and dab dry, then cut into slices. Mix lime juice, agave syrup, cachaça and triple sec. Crush ice cubes into big chunks. Place kumquats and ice cubes into a glass and add the alcohol mixture.

Preparation time: 15 minutes

Digestif

TANGERINE LIQUEUR

***

6 organic tangerines
4 organic oranges
6.7 fl. oz. (200 ml) triple sec
5 fl. oz. (150 ml) white rum
2 tbsp. sea buckthorn juice
½ cup (100 g) cane (brown) sugar

Wash tangerines and oranges with hot water and let cool. Use a grater to remove the zest from all of the fruit. Then extract the juice and mix with alcohol, sea buckthorn juice, sugar and zest and pour into a large bottle. Seal well. Store at room temperature for at least one week so the flavor can fully develop.

Preparation time: 30 minutes + 1 week storage time

Drink

ORANGE AND CARROT JUICE

***

8 oranges
14 oz. (400 g) carrots
1 drop canola oil

Squeeze oranges, wash carrots and press them through a juicer. Mix both juices and add a drop of canola oil. Serve immediately.

Preparation time: 15 minutes

INGREDIENTS

2.2 lb. (1 kg) Hokkaido or Japanese squash
4 orange bell peppers
3.3 lb. (600 g) carrots
3 large yams (sweet potatoes)
2 chili peppers
1 medium-sized onion
8 garlic cloves
1.7 oz. (50 g) fresh ginger

17 organic oranges
9 organic tangerines
8.8 oz. (125 g) kumquats
16 physalis
8 apricots
8 medlars
4 limes
1 lemon

2 cinnamon sticks
1 tsp. garam masala (Indian spice mix)
½ tsp. chili powder
1 tsp. ground turmeric
Salt
Freshly ground white pepper

1 small egg

5.2 oz. (150 g) Red Leicester cheese

1 tbsp. white balsamic vinegar
approx. 4 fl. oz. (120 ml) olive oil
8 tsp. orange olive oil
2 ½ tbsp. (40 ml) canola oil
1 tsp. pear mustard
3 tsp. medium hot or hot mustard (according to personal
taste)
2 tbsp. honey (e.g. orange blossom)
2 tbsp. unsweetened peanut butter
1 tsp. harissa paste (hot chili paste)
2 tsp. tomato paste
4 tbsp. agave syrup

7 oz. (200 g) red lentils
6 tbsp. flour
3 tbsp. bread crumbs
½ cup (120 g) + 1 tbsp. cane (brown) sugar
⅛ cup (30 g) white sugar

10.1 fl. oz. (100 ml) triple sec
3.4 fl. oz. (100 ml) cachaça
5 fl. oz. (150 ml) white rum
1 tbsp. dry white wine
2 tbsp. sea buckthorn juice

Ice cubes

01

02

03

04

01 Digestif   02 Drink   03 Main course   04 Appetizer

06

05

07

05 Apéritif 06 Dessert 07 Hors d'oeuvre

MENU
11

Apéritif
RED GRAPE JUICE

Appetizer
RED ONION SOUP

Hors d'oeuvre
RED VELVET SALAD WITH RASPBERRY DRESSING

Drink
RED WINE

Main course
STEAK WITH BORDELAISE SAUCE, BALSAMIC GLAZED POTATOES AND RED BEET (BEETROOT) CARPACCIO

Dessert
RED WINE SHERBET

Digestif
RED BERRY LIQUEUR

Appetizer

RED ONION SOUP

6.3 oz. (180 g) red onions

6.3 oz. (180 g) pre-cooked red beets (beetroots)

5 fl. oz. (150 ml) red wine

6.7 fl. oz. (200 ml) vegetable stock

1 ½ tsp. cane (brown) sugar

1 ½ tsp. raspberry vinegar

1 ½ tsp. lemon juice

Ground cumin

Red salt

Cayenne pepper

Sunflower oil

Peel onions and cut in half, then into thin slices. Heat some oil in a frying pan and sauté onions for approximately 10 minutes over medium heat. Finely dice about ⅓ of the red beets. Coarsely chop the remaining beets and purée with ⅓ of the sautéed onions and the wine in a blender. Sprinkle the sugar over the remaining onions in the frying pan and stir until they start to caramelize. Add the red wine mixture to deglaze. Next, pour in the vegetable stock and bring to a quick boil. Add the beet pieces and let simmer over low heat for about 5 minutes. Season with raspberry vinegar, lemon juice, salt, cayenne pepper and ground cumin.

Preparation time: 40 minutes

Hors d'oeuvre

RED VELVET SALAD WITH RASPBERRY DRESSING

5.5 oz. (100 g) radicchio
5.2 oz. (100 g) Lollo Rosso lettuce
5.2 oz. (100 g) red leaf lettuce
1 small pomegranate
1 handful red beet (beetroot) sprouts

DRESSING
¾ cup (100 g) raspberries, fresh or frozen
¼ cup (40 g) wild berries, frozen
1.5 tbsp. red grape juice
1.5 tbsp. raspberry vinegar
¼ cup (60 ml) olive oil
1 tsp. fig mustard
Red salt
Freshly ground black pepper

Bring berries and grape juice to a boil and simmer over low heat until berries fall apart. Pass through a sieve and add vinegar, oil and fig mustard. Whisk until dressing becomes smooth and thick, then season with salt and pepper.

Open the pomegranate and gently push out the seeds. Next, wash the radicchio, the red leaf lettuce and the Lollo Rosso and spin dry. Arrange on plates and top with the pomegranate seeds, sprouts and the dressing.

Preparation time: 20 minutes

Main course

STEAK WITH BORDELAISE SAUCE, BALSAMIC GLAZED POTATOES AND RED BEET (BEETROOT) CARPACCIO

RED BEET (BEETROOT) CARPACCIO

10.7 oz. (300 g) pre-cooked red beets (beetroots)
1 ½ tsp. raspberry vinegar
1 ½ tsp. red wine vinegar
4 tbsp. olive oil
1 ½ tsp. honey
1 ½ tsp. mustard (medium hot)
1 ½ tsp. horseradish
Red salt
Freshly ground black pepper

Slice beets paper-thin with a mandoline and arrange on a large plate. Season with salt and pepper. Mix vinegar, oil, honey and mustard. Season dressing with salt and pepper and drizzle over the carpaccio. Allow to infuse for 2 hours.

Preparation time: 20 minutes + 2 hours infusing time

BALSAMIC GLAZED POTATOES

1.5 lbs. (750 g) red potatoes
8 oz. (250 g) red onions
3 tbsp. olive oil
4 tbsp. balsamic vinegar
Red salt
Freshly ground black pepper

Preheat oven to 400 °F/200 °C/gas 6. Cut potatoes into bite-sized pieces. Peel onions and cut into eighths. In an ovenproof casserole dish, combine onions and potatoes and spread with olive oil. Cover with aluminum foil and bake for 30 minutes. Remove foil and turn up the heat to 450 °F/230 °C/gas 8. Add the remaining ingredients, stir well and bake for another 30 minutes, stirring occasionally. The potatoes are ready when the sides look golden brown and crunchy.

Preparation time: 15 minutes + 1 hour baking time

STEAK

4 beef steaks, about 5.6 oz. (160 g) each
Ghee or clarified butter
Red salt
Freshly grounded black pepper

SAUCE

13.5 fl. oz. (400 ml) red wine, e.g. Bordeaux
13.5 fl. oz. (400 ml) meat stock, e.g. veal stock
2 tbsp. cranberry juice (use juice from canned cranberries)
4 scallions
6 black peppercorns
1 sprig thyme
1 bay leaf
Red salt
Freshly ground black pepper
Cold butter

For the steak, melt ghee in the pan and fry the steaks until cooked medium (approx. 3–4 minutes each side), then cut the steaks into pieces and season with salt and pepper. Serve with the sauce, balsamic potatoes and the red beet carpaccio.

For the sauce, finely dice the scallions. In a frying pan, heat scallions, peppercorns, thyme, bay leaf and the red wine and bring to a boil, then lower the heat and allow sauce to reduce. Next, add the meat stock and the cranberry juice, stir well and bring to a boil. Over low heat, allow the sauce to reduce by ⅔. Season with salt and pepper and then pass the sauce through a fine sieve. Add a piece of cold butter to thicken the sauce.

Preparation time: 40 minutes

Total preparation time:
75 minutes + 1 hour baking time + 2 hours infusing time

Dessert

RED WINE SHERBET

6.7 fl. oz. (200 ml) dry red wine
6.7 fl. oz. (200 ml) dark red sparkling lemonade,
e.g. red grape or red berry lemonade
1 cup (200 g) sugar
6.7 fl. oz. (200 ml) still mineral water
1 organic lemon
3.5 oz. (100 g) seedless red grapes

In a saucepan, combine sugar and mineral water. Bring to a boil over medium heat and stir until sugar dissolves. Continue to simmer and stir for about 5 minutes until the mixture thickens to a syrup and then remove from heat. Wash the lemon with hot water and grate the zest, cut the lemon in two, and squeeze out the juice. In a large bowl, mix red wine and lemonade, add lemon zest, then lemon juice and the syrup. Stir well. Next, cover the mixture with plastic wrap and put it in the freezer for about 10 hours. For the first 2 hours, stir the mixture every 15 minutes, then freeze until firm.

Just before serving, use a hand-held blender and blend until the sherbet looks fluffy. Garnish each sherbet serving with red grapes.

Preparation time: 30 minutes + 10 hours freezing time

Digestif

RED BERRY LIQUEUR

1.1 lb. (500 g) mixed berries, fresh or frozen, e.g. blueberries,
blackberries, raspberries
25.3 fl. oz. (750 ml) raspberry schnapps (40%)
1 cup (200 g) cane (brown) sugar
½ cinnamon stick
1 vanilla bean

Slightly mash thawed berries and place into a large canning jar (use one with a lid). Slice open the vanilla bean length-wise and scrape seeds into the jar. Add the bean pod and the rest of the ingredients. Add the liqueur to the mixture and firmly seal the jar. Shake lightly and store the jar in a cool place for at least two months, making sure to shake the liquid every once in a while. Strain liqueur through a sieve into glasses and serve.

Preparation time:
20 minutes + 2 months storage time

Apéritif

RED GRAPE JUICE

At least 33.8 fl. oz. (1 l) red grape juice

Serve cold.

Drink

RED WINE

At least 1 bottle dry red wine

INGREDIENTS

1 lb. (480 g) pre-cooked red beets (beetroots)

1.5 lbs. (750 g) red potatoes

5.5 oz. (100 g) radicchio

5.2 oz. (100 g) Lollo Rosso lettuce

5.2 oz. (100 g) red leaf lettuce

14.3 oz. (430 g) red onions

4 scallions

1 handful red beet (beetroot) sprouts

1 sprig thyme

1 small pomegranate

3.5 oz. (100 g) seedless red grapes

1.2 lb. (540 g) mixed berries, fresh or frozen,
e.g. blueberries, blackberries, raspberries

$\frac{3}{4}$ cup (100 g) raspberries, fresh or frozen

2 organic lemons

1 bay leaf

Ground cumin

Cayenne pepper

$\frac{1}{2}$ cinnamon stick

1 vanilla bean

Red salt

6 black peppercorns

Freshly ground black pepper

4 beef steaks, about 5.6 oz. (160 g) each

Butter

Ghee or clarified butter

13.5 fl. oz. (400 ml) meat stock, e.g. veal stock

6.7 fl. oz. (200 ml) vegetable stock

$\frac{3}{4}$ cup (180 ml) olive oil

Sunflower oil

4 tbsp. balsamic vinegar

4 tbsp. raspberry vinegar

1.5 tsp. red wine vinegar

2 tbsp. cranberry juice (use juice from canned cranberries)

1 $\frac{1}{2}$ tsp. honey

1 $\frac{1}{2}$ tsp. mustard (medium hot)

1 $\frac{1}{2}$ tsp. horseradish

1 tsp. fig mustard

1 cup (200 g) sugar

1 cup (200 g) + 1 $\frac{1}{2}$ tsp. cane (brown) sugar

25.3 fl. oz. (750 ml) raspberry schnapps (40%)

2 bottles dry red wine, e.g. Bordeaux

6.7 fl. oz. (200 ml) dark red sparkling lemonade, e.g. red grape
or red berry lemonade

33.8 fl. oz. (1 l) red grape juice

6.7 fl. oz. (200 ml) still mineral water

01

02

03

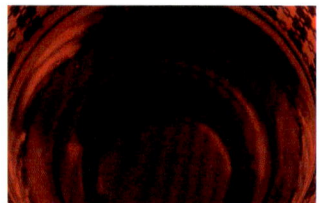

04

01 Main course 02 Dessert 03 Apéritif 04 Digestif

05

06

07

05 Drink 06 Hors d'oeuvre 07 Appetizer

MENU

12

Apéritif
SPICED TEA

Appetizer
**SWEET AND SPICY
CANDIED NUTS**

Hors d'oeuvre
**GALETTE WITH
MUSHROOM RAGOUT**

Drink
GERMAN ALTBIER

Main course
**VENISON ROAST WITH
GINGERBREAD SAUCE,
PUMPERNICKEL DUMPLINGS
AND MARINATED PEAR WITH
DATE CHUTNEY**

Dessert
MI-CUIT AU CHOCOLAT

Digestif
ESPRESSO

Appetizer

SWEET AND SPICY
CANDIED NUTS

2.8 oz. (80 g) almonds

2.8 oz. (80 g) hazelnuts

2.8 oz. (80 g) walnuts

2.8 oz. (80 g) pecans

1.4 oz. (40 g) cane (brown) sugar

1 pinch ground cloves

½ tsp. ground cinnamon

¼ tsp. cayenne pepper

¼ tsp. ground cumin

½ tsp. salt

¼ tsp. freshly ground black pepper

Preheat oven to 350 °F/180 °C/gas 4. Spread nuts on a baking tray lined with parchment paper and bake for 5 to 10 minutes until crunchy. Let cool. In a bowl, mix sugar and spices. Heat a frying pan and add the baked nuts and the sugar-spice mixture. While sugar liquefies, roast nuts for about 5 to 10 minutes over medium heat, stirring constantly and shaking the pan gently every once in a while. Next, spread the sugar-coated nuts on a sheet of parchment paper. Use a fork to separate the nuts that stick together. Cool before serving.

Preparation time: 30 minutes

Hors d'oeuvre

GALETTE WITH MUSHROOM RAGOUT

FILLING
1.8 oz. (250 g) brown mushrooms
4.2 fl. oz. (125 ml) dry sherry
2 tbsp. white wine vinegar
4.2 fl. oz. (125 ml) water
2 sprigs thyme
2 bay leaves
1 garlic clove
2 scallions
3 tbsp. butter
½ tsp. salt
Freshly ground black pepper

DOUGH (MAKES 4 GALETTES)
7.9 oz. (225 g) buckwheat flour
0.8 oz. (25 g) whole grain flour
1.7 oz. (50 g) butter
2 small eggs
8.4 fl. oz. (250 ml) cold water
Salt

For the dough, in a bowl, combine flour, salt, eggs and cold water. Add the melted butter and mix to a smooth, liquid batter (it should run off easily when poured from a spoon). Let dough cool for 2 hours.

In the meantime, wash mushrooms. Cut off the stems and set aside. Cut the mushroom heads into fine slices. Peel and dice scallions and garlic, add to a saucepan and sauté with 1 tbsp. of butter until translucent. Add the sherry and then the 4.2 fl. oz. (⅛ l) of water, white wine vinegar, mushroom stems, thyme and bay leaves and simmer for 15 minutes. Pass through a fine sieve into another saucepan, pressing down firmly on the solids to extract a stock. Heat the remaining butter and sauté mushroom slices until done. Mix with the stock. Season ragout with salt and pepper. Add extra butter to taste.

Preheat oven to 122 °F/50 °C/gas 1. Heat a non-stick frying pan and grease with a small piece of butter. Next, add small amounts of batter to the pan. Quickly tilt and rotate the pan to swirl the butter and spread it as evenly as possible. When the bottom is slightly browned, turn the galette and briefly cook the other side until brown. Stack the baked galettes on a plate and place them in the preheated oven to keep warm. Heat up the ragout. Fill each galette with ragout and serve.

Preparation time: 1 hour + 2 hours standing time

VENISON ROAST

2.2 lb. (1 kg) venison loin

5 thin slices of bacon

1 large red onion

2 carrots

$\frac{1}{6}$ celeriac

1 small parsley root

$\frac{1}{2}$ leek

2 bay leaves

2 juniper berries

2 allspice seeds

Salt

Freshly ground black pepper

Olive oil

Marinade (for the meat)

8.4 fl. oz. (250 ml) red wine vinegar

1 large onion

3 garlic cloves

10 juniper berries

5 allspice seeds

$\frac{1}{2}$ tsp. mustard seeds

$\frac{1}{2}$ tsp. coriander seeds

5 bay leaves

8.4 fl. oz. (250 ml) water

Game Stock

1 lb. (500 g) game meat

1 lb. (500 g) game bones

3 carrots

$\frac{1}{2}$ celeriac

1 parsley root

2 leeks

1 large onion

2 garlic cloves

50.7 fl. oz. (1.5 l) water

$1\frac{1}{2}$ tsp. salt

Freshly ground black pepper

Olive oil

GINGERBREAD SAUCE

1.7 oz. (50 g) gingerbread

8.4 fl. oz. (250 ml) dry red wine

$\frac{1}{2}$ tsp. gingerbread spice

Salt

Freshly ground black pepper

Main course

VENISON ROAST WITH GINGERBREAD SAUCE, PUMPERNICKEL DUMPLINGS AND MARINATED PEAR WITH DATE CHUTNEY

For the marinade, peel and coarsely chop garlic. Peel onions and cut into large chunks. In a big bowl, combine red wine vinegar with water. Add chopped garlic cloves, onion chunks and spices. Place the whole venison roast in the marinade and make sure it is evenly covered by the liquid. Let marinate for 2 days in a cool place.

For the game stock, coarsely chop celeriac, leek, parsley root, onions and garlic (both with the peel). In a large saucepan, heat olive oil. Add game meat, bones and the vegetables and briefly fry over high heat. Next, add 50.7 fl. oz. (1.5 l) of water. Reduce heat, season with salt and pepper and let simmer for 1 hour or until liquid has reduced by one half. Strain stock and set aside.

Preheat oven to 338 °F/170 °C/gas 3–4. Remove the venison roast from the marinade and dab dry with paper towels. Cut the red onion (with the skin) into quarters and briefly fry in a roasting pan. Add venison loin and sear on all sides. Coarsely chop the vegetables and add to the roasting pan, then add the seeds, bay leaves, salt and pepper. Next, add the prepared game stock (cover about ⅓ of the roast with the stock). Set aside 3.4 fl. oz. (100 ml) of stock because you will need it later to keep the roast moist. Spread bacon across the top of the venison and place in the preheated oven (do not cover with a lid!). After 45 minutes, pour the remaining stock over the roast, then cover with a lid and roast for about 60 minutes. If the meat is not done, roast for 30 more minutes. Finally, remove venison from the pan, wrap it in aluminum foil and keep it in a warm place for 10 minutes. Strain the stock from the roast pan and to save for the gingerbread sauce.

For the sauce, crumble gingerbread. Pour the stock into a saucepan and add the red wine and gingerbread spice. Bring to a boil and simmer for 10 minutes or until the liquid has reduced and thickened and the gingerbread has fully dissolved. Purée sauce and season with salt and pepper.

Carve roast into slices and serve with gingerbread sauce, pumpernickel dumplings and marinated pear.

Preparation time:
3 hours + 1.5 hours baking time + 2 days marinating time

PUMPERNICKEL DUMPLINGS
7 oz. (200 g) pumpernickel bread
1.8 oz. (50 g) brazil nuts
1 mealy potato
1 red onion
1 egg
Freshly ground nutmeg
Salt
Freshly ground black pepper
Sunflower oil
Some milk (as required)

Cook potato, cool and peel, then mash with a fork. Crumble pumpernickel bread into tiny pieces. Finely chop brazil nuts and mix with the potato and the pumpernickel. Peel and dice onion and sauté in oil until translucent. Next, knead pumpernickel mixture, onions and egg to form a dough and season with nutmeg, salt and pepper. Add some milk, if needed. Using your hands, shape into four dumplings. Tightly wrap the dumplings in aluminum foil and cook for 30 minutes in boiling water. Let dumplings cool off a bit before serving.

Preparation time: 1 hour

MARINATED PEAR
2 firm ripe pears
8.4 fl. oz. (250 ml) red wine
1.7 fl. oz. (50 ml) red balsamic vinegar
2 cloves
½ tsp. cinnamon
½ tsp. cane (brown) sugar
Salt

Peel the pears and cut into halves. Remove the cores and the stems. In a wide saucepan, heat red wine, vinegar and the spices. Add the pear halves and simmer for 20 minutes over medium heat, turning them over occasionally. Remove the saucepan from the stove and let cool before removing the pears from the liquid (save the liquid). Stuff the pears with the date chutney. Heat the liquid in the saucepan until it has thickened. Before serving, drizzle the stuffed pear halves with the sauce.

Preparation time: 45 minutes

DATE CHUTNEY
4 dried, juicy dates
4 dried figs
3 tbsp. (30 g) sultanas
4.3 fl. oz. (130 ml) white balsamic vinegar
2 tbsp. (30 ml) elderflower syrup
⅓ cup (60 g) cane (brown) sugar
2 scallions
½ tsp. fresh ginger
1 cinnamon stick
2 cardamom pods
¼ tsp. ground coriander
¼ tsp. cayenne pepper
½ tsp. salt

Remove the pits from the dates and peel. Dice dates and figs and mix with sultanas in a bowl. Peel and dice scallions. Peel and grate ginger and add to the bowl. In a saucepan, bring vinegar, sugar and elderflower syrup to a boil. Add the dried-fruit mixture, scallions, ginger, cinnamon stick and cardamom pods, bring to a boil again and simmer for 30 minutes. Season with coriander, salt and cayenne pepper. Stir well and let cool.

Preparation time: 1 hour

Total preparation time:
5 hours and 45 minutes + 1.5 hours baking time
+ 2 days marinating time

Dessert

MI-CUIT AU CHOCOLAT

3.1 oz. (90 g) dark chocolate
2.6 oz. (75 g) cold butter
2 tbsp. (20 g) butter
2 tbsp. white spelt flour
3 small eggs
5 tbsp. cane (brown) sugar
1 vanilla bean
Cocoa powder

4 soufflé dishes (Ø 3.1 inch/8 cm)

Grease the soufflé dishes with butter and dust with flour. Preheat oven to 450 °F/ 230 °C/gas 8. In a small bowl, add finely chopped chocolate and melt with butter over a bain marie. Slice the vanilla bean lengthwise and scrape out the seeds. Separate 1 egg. In a bowl, beat egg yolk with the remaining two eggs, sugar and vanilla seeds. Add the melted chocolate and 1 ½ tbsp. of flour. Pour into dishes and bake for approximately 8 to 9 minutes. Frequently check the soufflés – they are done when the dough on top starts to close up. The soufflés need to be firm on the outside, but liquid on the inside. Carefully invert the soufflés dishes onto plates. Let them cool upside down for 15 seconds, and then remove the dishes from the soufflés. Carefully turn soufflés over again and dust with cocoa powder. Serve immediately.

Preparation time:
20 minutes + 10 minutes baking time

Apéritif

SPICED TEA

---

1 cinnamon stick
2 star aniseed
5 cardamom pods
5 cloves
5 allspice seeds
Freshly ground black pepper
$\frac{1}{3}$ oz. (10 g) fresh ginger
50.7 fl. oz. (1.5 l) water
Maple syrup

Peel and grate ginger. In a saucepan, combine ginger with the other spices and add 50.7 fl. oz. (1.5 l) of water. Bring to a boil and let simmer for 25 minutes or until the tea has reduced to 33.8 fl. oz. (1 l). Pour into 4 large glasses and sweeten to taste with maple syrup.

Preparation time: 30 minutes

Digestif

ESPRESSO

Espresso (light roast)
$\frac{1}{3}$ cup (80 ml) heavy (double) cream

Top off coffee with 1 tbsp. of cream per cup.

Preparation time: 10 minutes

Drink

GERMAN ALTBIER

---

4 bottles

Serve cool.

INGREDIENTS

1.8 oz. (250 g) brown mushrooms

$\frac{2}{3}$ celeriac

2 parsley roots

2 $\frac{1}{2}$ leeks

1 mealy potato

2 large red onions

2 large onions

4 scallions

6 garlic cloves

5 carrots

$\frac{1}{2}$ oz. (15 g) fresh ginger

2 sprigs thyme

2 firm ripe pears

9 bay leaves

12 juniper berries

12 allspice seeds

7 cloves

7 cardamom pods

$\frac{1}{2}$ tsp. coriander seeds

$\frac{1}{2}$ tsp. mustard seeds

2 cinnamon sticks

2 star aniseed

1 pinch ground cloves

1 tsp. ground cinnamon

$\frac{1}{4}$ tsp. ground coriander

$\frac{1}{4}$ tsp. ground cumin

$\frac{1}{2}$ tsp. cayenne pepper

Freshly ground nutmeg

$\frac{1}{2}$ tsp. gingerbread spice

1 vanilla bean

Salt

Freshly ground black pepper

2.2 lb. (1 kg) venison loin

1 lb. (500 g) game meat

1 lb. (500 g) game bones

5 thin slices of bacon

6 small eggs

$\frac{1}{3}$ cup (80 ml) heavy (double) cream

7 oz. (200 g) butter

Some milk (as required)

Olive oil

Sunflower oil

8.4 fl. oz. (250 ml) red wine vinegar

2 tbsp. white wine vinegar

1.7 fl. oz. (50 ml) red balsamic vinegar

4.3 fl. oz. (130 ml) white balsamic vinegar

2 tbsp. (30 ml) elderflower syrup

Maple syrup

Espresso (light roast)

7.9 oz. (225 g) buckwheat flour

0.8 oz. (25 g) whole grain flour

2 tbsp. white spelt flour

2.8 oz. (80 g) almonds

2.8 oz. (80 g) hazelnuts

2.8 oz. (80 g) walnuts

2.8 oz. (80 g) pecans

1.8 oz. (50 g) brazil nuts

4 dried, juicy dates

4 dried figs

3 tbsp. (30 g) sultanas

7.4 oz. (210 g) cane (brown) sugar

3.1 oz. (90 g) dark chocolate

Cocoa powder

1.7 oz. (50 g) gingerbread

7 oz. (200 g) pumpernickel bread

16.9 fl. oz. (500 ml) red wine

4.2 fl. oz. (125 ml) dry sherry

4 bottles German Altbier

4 soufflé dishes (Ø 3.1 inch/8 cm)

01

02

03

01 Appetizer 02 Digestif 03 Dessert

04

05

06

07

04 Apéritif 05 Drink 06 Main course 07 Hors d'oeuvre

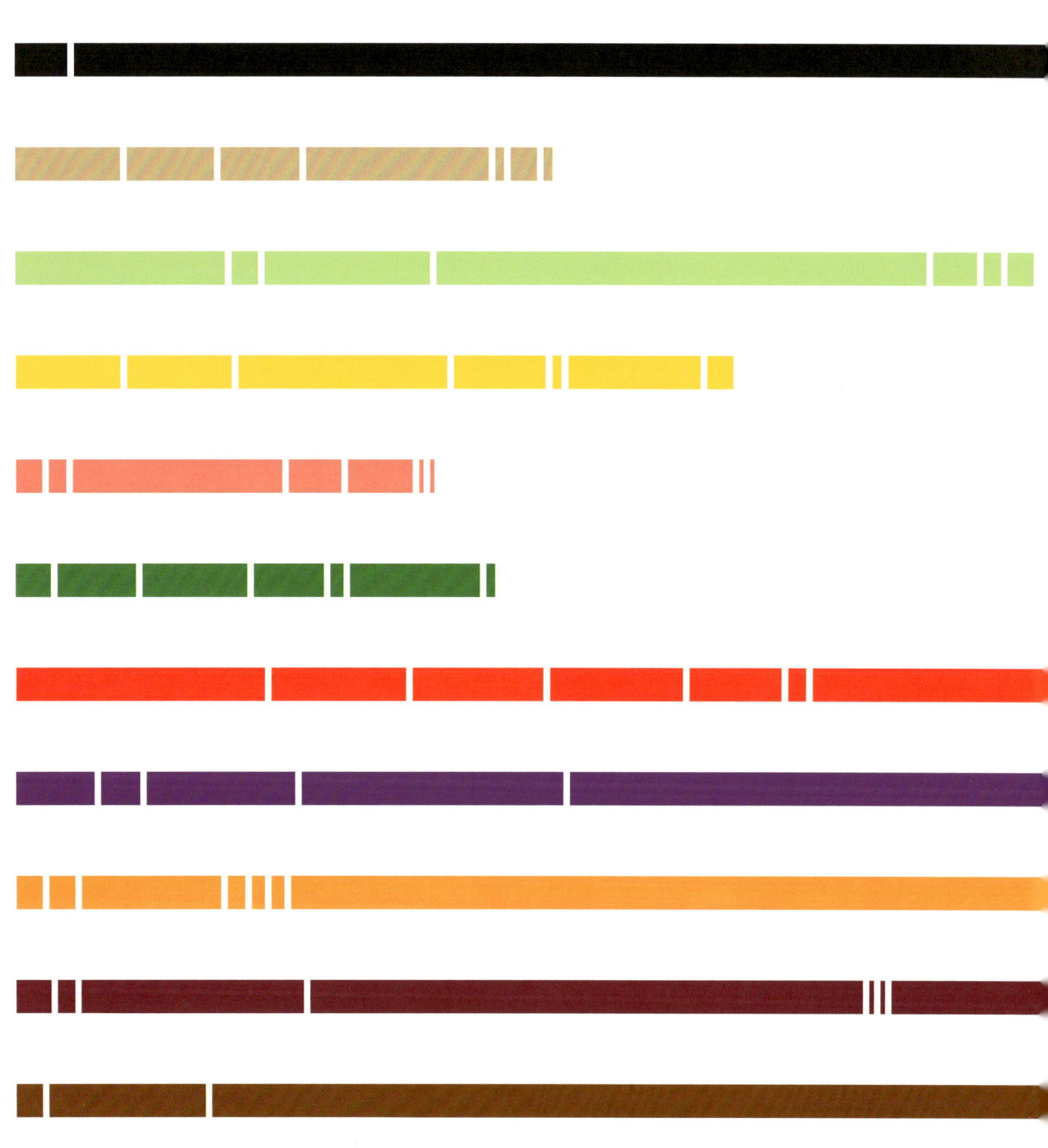

PREPARATION TIME ▸ Appetizer + Hors d'oeuvre + Main course + Dessert + Apéritif + Drink + Digestif

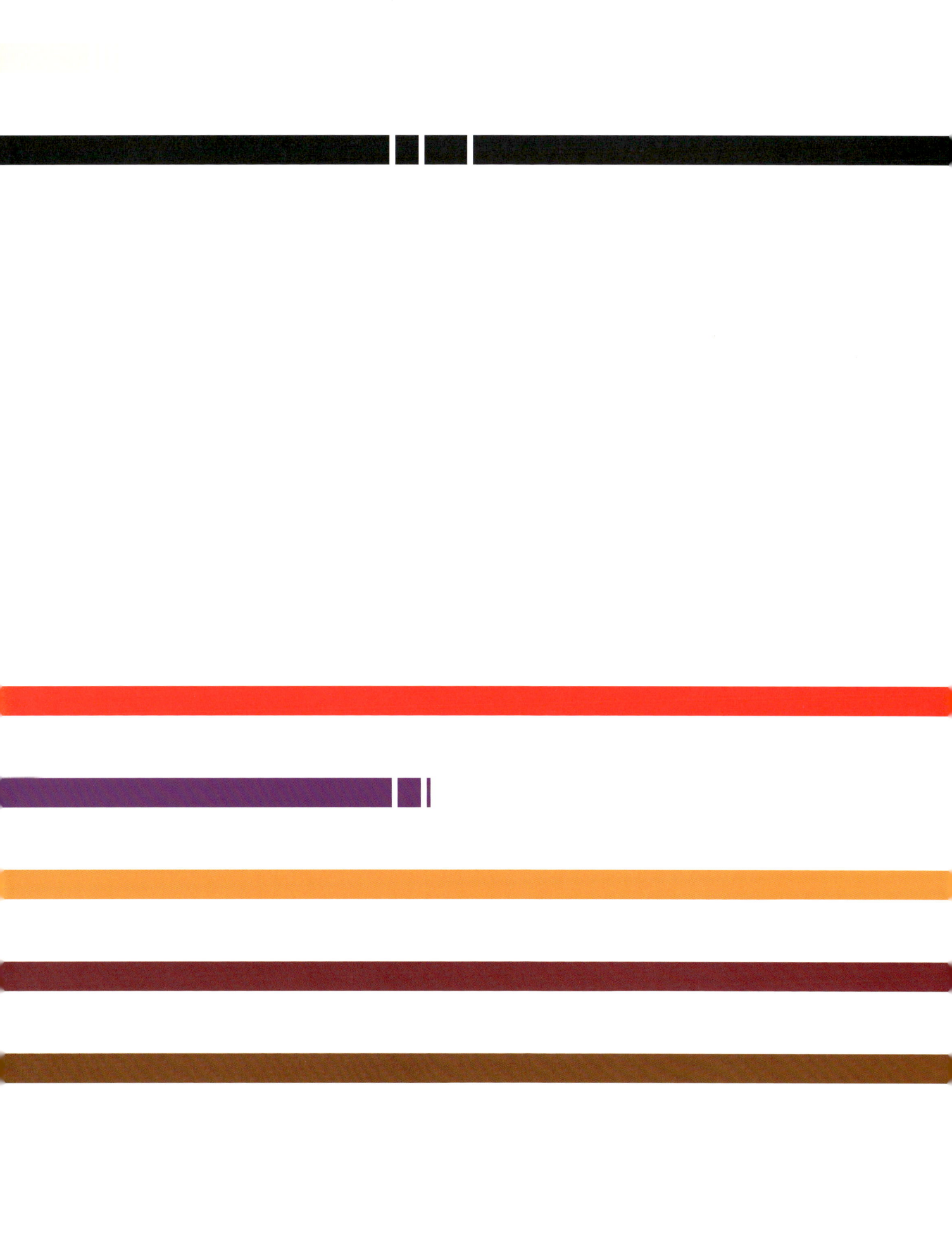

MENUS

EPILOGUE

We really hope that our twelve color-coded menus inspire you to cook monochromatic meals that you relish.

In the following section, we have listed a few more points about the menus.

All menus were created and photographed without any artificial colors. Please keep in mind that the dishes may vary in color and taste depending on the quality of the ingredients and where they were bought. We urge you to carefully choose your ingredients and try your best to match each ingredient to the menu color. The closer the match, the better the results.

Certainly, the priority here is the color theme. The goal is to have the best color matching and the most monochromatic menu. However, to guarantee diverse and complete menus (which was very important to us), we sometimes had to use other colored ingredients. Also, it wasn't always possible to follow our theme using just seasonal ingredients. Since some fresh ingredients change color or lose their flavor when cooked, occasionally, we used frozen or preserved products. For example, a colored dough will almost entirely lose its color while baking.

Some colors are harder to achieve than others, especially violet. Most violet foods will turn reddish or brownish when being prepared. True violet ingredients are rare since they hardly exist in nature. In this case, the color really depends on the preparation process. For example, red cabbage is reddish or blueish (in Germany, it is also called "Blaukraut," meaning blue cabbage), depending on the region and the type of soil it grows in.

Some ingredients have the desired color when they are raw, while others need to be prepared in a certain way before they turn the right shade (by marinating, concentrating, filtering or extracting). What this means, for example, is that in the yellow menu, you don't necessarily need to use only yellow ingredients, but as many yellow ingredients as possible in order to achieve a final monochromatic meal.

The color of the ingredients often dictates the taste. For that reason, the list of spices used in the brown menu, for example, is quite long, resulting in a very flavorful meal. It is the same with the light red menu, where the flavor is influenced by the versatility of the ingredients' aromas. In the dark green menu, the variety of herbs impacts the final result. Sometimes, we discovered, the color simply suggests a flavor. For example, although the lavender lemonade is translucent, the flavor is so intense it tastes violet!

Cooking monochromatic menus means experimenting with different flavors, colors and looks – almost like in a laboratory. This method is sure to sharpen your senses and give you a new appreciation of cooking.

SPECIAL THANKS

Special thanks to our highly motivated smutjes,
chefs, diners, and helpers-of-all-sorts who have contributed
so much to this project. This book would not
be the same without their input, ideas, culinary skills,
know-how and inspirations:

Lene Marie Gotholdt, Sonja Hornung,
Lisa Kirfel-Rühle, Bettina Lamprecht, Trish Lorenz,
Dušanka Maličević, Julia Masagão, Uli Meyer,
Uta Schrameyer, Lisa Seibert, Claudia Thybusch,
Alexandra Wetzel, Karin Wolfram

Extra special thanks must go to all the employees from
Prestel Verlag, who helped us to realize this book,
particularly **Claudia Stäuble**, who was our first contact and
who believed in our project from the start; **Julie Kiefer**,
who remained steadfastly committed throughout mounting
challenges; and the **teams of test cooks**, who supported
us and sacrificed their well-deserved time-off to try out our
recipes and provide valuable feedback.

Many thanks!

ABOUT THE AUTHORS

Architect and product designer **Iatjana Reimann** is
the co-founder of the label "kolor Studio für Gestaltung"
in Berlin (www.kolor.de). As an artist, she loves anything
that challenges her in a creative way.
WWW.TATJANAREIMANN.COM

For over ten years, the designers
Caro Mantke and Tim Schober have been working in
communication design, interactive design and illustration as
"MS MANTOBER." Besides their day-to-day business, they
are passionately involved in their own art projects.
WWW.MS-MANTOBER.DE

INGREDIENTS INDEX

LOVAGE
SWISS CHARD ROLLS WITH
    HERBED CREAM SAUCE –107

MACADAMIA NUTS
JERUSALEM ARTICHOKE PIZZA –43

MANGOS
MANGO LASSI –79

MAPLE SYRUP
SPICED TEA –191

MASCARPONE
BLUEBERRY TARTELETTES –142
CAULIFLOWER RISOTTO –12

MATCHA GREEN TEA POWDER
GREEN BROWNIES –110
GREEN TEA ICE CREAM –62

MEAT STOCK
BORDELAISE SAUCE –173

MEDLARS
CARAMELIZED FRUIT –158

MILK
CAFÉ AU LAIT –47
CAULIFLOWER CREAM SAUCE –12
GREEN TEA ICE CREAM WITH
    PISTACHIO COOKIES –62
MANGO LASSI –79
RAVIOLI –76
SALTY LASSI –15
SWISS CHARD ROLLS –107
VIOLET SMOOTHIE –143

MINCED MEAT
SEE GROUND MEAT

MINERAL WATER
GINGER LEMONADE –79
GREEN GRAPE LEMONADE –63
LAVENDER LEMONADE –143
MANGO LASSI –79
PEPPERMINT LEMONADE –111
RED WINE SHERBET –174
RHUBARB SPRITZER –95
TRIPLE GREEN MOJITO –63
WHITE WINE SPRITZER –15

MUSHROOMS
SEE BUTTON MUSHROOMS,
ENOKI MUSHROOMS, PORCINI

MUSTARD
SEE ALSO FIG MUSTARD,
PEAR MUSTARD
ORANGE MUSTARD
    VINAIGRETTE –154
RED BEET (BEETROOT)
    CARPACCIO –172
TAPENADE –28

MUSTARD SEEDS
VENISON ROAST –188

NECTARINES
SANGRIA –127

NORI LEAVES
MAKI SUSHI –27

NUTMEG
BROWN RICE –44
PARSNIP SOUP –11
PUMPERNICKEL DUMPLINGS –189
RED CABBAGE SOUP –138
SWISS CHARD ROLLS WITH
    HERBED CREAM SAUCE –107

OLIVES
SEE ALSO GEMLIK OLIVES
(BLACK) BELUGA LENTIL SALAD –26
(GREEN) OLIVE PESTO –60

ONIONS
SEE ALSO PEARL ONIONS,
SCALLIONS, SPRING ONIONS
BELUGA LENTIL SALAD –26
BLUE TORTILLAS –140
BROWN RICE –44
GREEN TOMATO SAUCE –108
MUSHROOM SOUP –42
RED CABBAGE SOUP –138
RED LENTIL PATTIES –157
RHUBARB RELISH –92
STUFFED BELL PEPPERS –124
TORTILLA WITH MOJO
    AMARILLO –74
VEGETABLE STOCK –58
VENISON ROAST –188
(RED) BALSAMIC GLAZED
    POTATOES –172
(RED) PUMPERNICKEL
    DUMPLINGS –189
(RED) RED BEET (BEETROOT)
    RISOTTO –92
(RED) RED ONION SOUP –170
(WHITE) CAULIFLOWER RISOTTO –12
(WHITE) PARSNIP SOUP –11
(WHITE) WHITE WINE SAUCE –13
(WHITE) YELLOW LENTIL SOUP –75

ORANGE JUICE
MAI TAI –79
MOJO AMARILLO –74

ORANGE OLIVE OIL
STEWED PUMPKIN –156
SWEET POTATO SOUP –155

ORANGES
SEE ALSO BLOOD ORANGES
ORANGE AND CARROT JUICE –159
ORANGE MUSTARD
    VINAIGRETTE –154
PEPPERMINT LEMONADE –111
STEWED PUMPKIN –156
SWEET POTATO SOUP –155
TANGERINE LIQUEUR –159

OREGANO
SALSA –140

PARMESAN CHEESE
CAULIFLOWER RISOTTO –12
RAVIOLI –76
RED BEET (BEETROOT) RISOTTO –92
SPINACH LASAGNE –108
ZUCCHINI (COURGETTE)
    CARPACCIO –60

PARSLEY
SWISS CHARD ROLLS WITH
    HERBED CREAM SAUCE –107

PARSLEY ROOTS
GAME STOCK –188
PARSNIP SOUP –11
SUMMER ROLLS –10
VEGETABLE STOCK
    –42, 58, 75, 92, 124, 138

PARSNIPS
PARSNIP SOUP –11
SUMMER ROLLS –10
VEGETABLE STOCK –58, 124, 138
YELLOW LENTIL SOUP –75

PASTIS –15

PEANUT BUTTER (UNSWEETENED)
SWEET POTATO SOUP –155

PEANUT OIL
VIOLET POTATO CHIPS –139

PEAR MUSTARD
ORANGE MUSTARD
    VINAIGRETTE –154

PEARL ONIONS –12

PEARS
MARINATED PEAR –189
RED CABBAGE SOUP –138

PECANS
CANDIED NUTS –186

PEPPERMINT
PEPPERMINT LEMONADE –111
SWISS CHARD ROLLS –107
TRIPLE GREEN MOJITO –63

PEPPERS
SEE BELL PEPPERS

PESTO CHEESE
SPINACH LASAGNE –108

PHYSALIS
CARAMELIZED FRUIT –158

PINE NUTS
JERUSALEM ARTICHOKE PIZZA –43
RAVIOLI WITH BELL PEPPER AND
    RICOTTA FILLING –76

PINEAPPLE JUICE
MAI TAI –79

PINEAPPLES
PEPPERMINT LEMONADE –111
YELLOW LENTIL SOUP –75

PINK GRAPEFRUIT
SALMON FILET WITH PINK
    HORSERADISH CRUST –93

PISTACHIOS
OLIVE PESTO –60
PISTACCIO COOKIES –62
PISTACHIO-CILANTRO
    (CORIANDER) MEATBALLS –106
SPINACH LASAGNE –108

POMEGRANATE
RED VELVET SALAD –171

POPPY SEEDS
POPPY SEED CAKE –30

PORCINI (DRIED)
MUSHROOM SOUP –42

PORK STEAKS
STIR-FRIED PORK STEAKS –44

PORT WINE (RED)
SANGRIA –127

POTATOES
MUSHROOM SOUP –42
PUMPERNICKEL DUMPLINGS –189
(PURPLE) BLUE TORTILLAS –140
(PURPLE) VIOLET POTATO
    CHIPS –139
(RED) BALSAMIC GLAZED
    POTATOES –172
(YELLOW) TORTILLA WITH
    MOJO AMARILLO –74
(YELLOW) YELLOW LENTIL
    SOUP –75

POWDERED SUGAR
MERINGUE –14

PRAWNS –93

PROSECCO
KIWI LIME PUNCH –63

PRUNES (SOFT, BLACK)
TAPENADE –28

PUMPERNICKEL
PUMPERNICKEL DUMPLINGS –189

PUMPKIN SEED OIL
ARUGULA (ROCKET) SALAD –106

PUMPKIN SEEDS
SPINACH LASAGNE –108

RADICCHIO
RED VELVET SALAD –171

RADISH
SUMMER ROLLS –10

RADISH (BLACK)
MAKI SUSHI –27

RADISH SPROUTS (RED)
BLUE TORTILLAS –140

RAPESEED (CANOLA) HONEY
GREEN ASPARAGUS SALAD –59

RASPBERRIES
RASPBERRY DRESSING –171

RASPBERRY SCHNAPPS
RED BERRY LIQUEUR –175

RASPBERRY VINEGAR
RASPBERRY DRESSING –171
RED BEET (BEETROOT)
    CARPACCIO –172
RED ONION SOUP –170

RED BEET (BEETROOT) JUICE
STRAWBERRY AND CREAM
    SWISS ROLL –94

RED BEET (BEETROOT) SPROUTS
RED VELVET SALAD –171

RED BEETS (BEETROOTS)
RED BEET (BEETROOT)
    CARPACCIO –172
RED BEET (BEETROOT) RISOTTO –92
RED ONION SOUP –170

© PRESTEL VERLAG, MUNICH · LONDON · NEW YORK, 2014

PRESTEL VERLAG, MUNICH
A MEMBER OF VERLAGSGRUPPE RANDOM HOUSE GMBH

PRESTEL VERLAG
NEUMARKTER STRASSE 28
81673 MUNICH
TEL. +49 (0)89 4136-0
FAX +49 (0)89 4136-2335

PRESTEL PUBLISHING LTD.
14-17 WELLS STREET
LONDON W1T 3PD
TEL. +44 (0)20 7323-5004
FAX +44 (0)20 7323-0271

PRESTEL PUBLISHING
900 BROADWAY, SUITE 603
NEW YORK, NY 10003
TEL. +1 (212) 995-2720
FAX +1 (212) 995-2733

WWW.PRESTEL.COM

LIBRARY OF CONGRESS CONTROL NUMBER: 2013956203;
BRITISH LIBRARY CATALOGUING-IN-PUBLICATION DATA:
A CATALOGUE RECORD FOR THIS BOOK IS AVAILABLE FROM
THE BRITISH LIBRARY; DEUTSCHE NATIONALBIBLIOTHEK
HOLDS A RECORD OF THIS PUBLICATION IN THE DEUTSCHE
NATIONALBIBLIOGRAFIE; DETAILED BIBLIOGRAPHICAL
DATA CAN BE FOUND UNDER: HTTP://WWW.DNB.DE

PRESTEL BOOKS ARE AVAILABLE WORLDWIDE.
PLEASE CONTACT YOUR NEAREST BOOKSELLER OR
ONE OF THE ABOVE ADDRESSES FOR INFORMATION
CONCERNING YOUR LOCAL DISTRIBUTOR.

CONCEPT
TATJANA REIMANN & CARO MANTKE

RECIPE DEVELOPMENT & TESTING
TATJANA REIMANN & CARO MANTKE WITH COOKING TEAM

DESIGNED BY
CARO MANTKE, MS MANTOBER

TEXT
TATJANA REIMANN

PHOTOGRAPHY
TIM SCHOBER, MS MANTOBER

FOREWORD
TRISH LORENZ, FOOD AND DESIGN JOURNALIST

EDITORIAL DIRECTION
CLAUDIA STÄUBLE

PROJECT MANAGEMENT
JULIE KIEFER

TRANSLATION
ALEXANDRA DONATH

COPYEDITS
MEREDITH HAYS; TRISH LORENZ

PRODUCTION
ASTRID WEDEMEYER

SEPARATIONS
REPROLINE MEDIATEAM, MUNICH

PRINTING AND BINDING
NEOGRAFIA AG, MARTIN

PRINTED IN SLOVAKIA

VERLAGSGRUPPE RANDOM HOUSE FSC® N001967
THE FSC®-CERTIFIED PAPERS
PROFIMATT AND *MUNKEN PRINT WHITE*
WERE SUPPLIED BY IGEPA.

ISBN 978-3-7913-4899-5